If Only That
HORSE Were A
Member Of My
Church

*Anecdotes, Poems, and
Parables from the Lighter
Side of Church Life*

CHARLES W. BYRD

C.S.S. Publishing Co., Inc.

Lima, Ohio

IF ONLY THAT HORSE WERE A MEMBER

8821 / ISBN 1-55673-036-5   PRINTED IN U.S.A.

For my wife and my mother

If Only That
HORSE Were A
Member Of My
Church

Preface

This book was prepared to assist ministers and others who find themselves in need of a humorous or inspirational anecdote, sentence, or filler for a speech, sermon, newsletter or bulletin. I have also attempted to make it the kind of book which one might enjoy just for occasional reading.

Much of the material is original, taken from my own experiences and writings. The rest has been accumulated from a host of other sources over a period of many years. I have tried to give credit, where possible, for all material used.

It is my prayer that this small book might be of significant interest and help to all who chance to read it.

— Charles W. Byrd

(1) **In the Beginning**

In the beginning, God created the heaven and the earth. (Genesis 1:1)

Some years ago, I heard a noted astronomer speak at a college assembly on the subject of the origin of the universe. The lecturer began by declaring himself an atheist, and emphasized that his theory of creation did not include a Supreme Creator.

For an hour he presented a very convincing discourse on this theory. He spoke of the manner in which the earth and other heavenly bodies had been created by cosmic dust. But when he finished the lecture and asked for questions from the group, the obvious question was immediately asked by a young freshman.

"But, Professor, where did the cosmic dust come from?"

(2) **Flight of the Bumblebee**

According to the law of aerodynamics, the size of the bumblebee's body in relation to its wings makes it virtually impossible for the insect to fly. But the bumblebee apparently doesn't know this — and continues to buzz happily and confidently through the air. Yet it is not ignorance, but faith which allows us to accomplish the seemingly impossible. "With God, all things are possible." (Matthew 19:26)

10

(3)   *Preacher Clarkson Takes a Ride*

In the early days of railroading, Preacher Clarkson decided to take his first train ride on a visit to a neighboring town. He boarded the one-coach train and seated himself on a hard, wooden seat.

"First class, second class, or third class?" asked the conductor.

Clarkson had no idea what the man was talking about. "Which is cheapest?" he asked.

"Third class," answered the conductor as he wrote "3" on a black and white ticket.

Clarkson was bewildered as he watched the other passengers buying a mixture of the three tickets. His questions were answered however, when the small steam engine came to a shuddering halt on a steep grade.

"First class passengers, keep your seats!" yelled the conductor. "Second class passengers, get out and walk! Third class passengers, get out and push!"

(4)   *A Dime in Time*

The offering had been announced and the ushers began to move among the congregation. A lady sitting near the rear of the church dug through a pocketbook filled with keys, tissue, cosmetics, and numerous other items of stereotypical womanhood. As the ushers drew nearer, the woman became more frantic. A little boy sitting on the other end of the pew watched with intense interest. As the approach of the ushers became imminent, and the distress of the woman more apparent, the little boy scooted across the pew and whispered, "Here, lady, you take my dime. I can hide under the seat!"

(5)   A Mother's Faith

Once, while in Cuba I was asked to preach to a rural group far from a city. The appointed place was on a hilltop from which I could see for many miles. At the scheduled time, with the friendly faces looking up at me from their positions on the ground, I began to speak. My interpreter touched my arm and pointed into the growing darkness toward a lantern carried by someone moving toward us from the valley below.

The latecomer was a weary but radiant mother, carrying in her arms the disease-twisted form of her daughter. As the mother sat on the ground tenderly cradling the child, they both smiled up at me expectantly. I thought of the comforting words spoken by our Savior as he stood on a hillside long ago speaking to the expectant multitude.

> Blessed are they that mourn: for they shall be comforted. Blessed are they which do hunger and thirst after righteousness: for they shall be filled. Blessed are the pure in heart: for they shall see God.
>
> — Matthew 5

I had a very strong feeling that that mother and child had seen God a long time before, and were in communication with him every day.

(6)   Just Show Him Your Hands

A Kentucky bishop often told this story of an incident which occurred during his early ministry.

The young pastor's first appointment, in the early part of the century, was in the Appalachian mountain coal region. He was told of the serious illness of a fourteen-year-old girl who lived with her disabled father and two younger brothers in a remote valley cabin. The young preacher found the girl, lying on a cot in the barren three-room shanty. He had learned of the family's circumstance on his long walk through the mountains. The girl's father had been disabled in a mining accident, and her mother had died in childbirth three years before. Thus, at the age of eleven, the young girl had been thrust into the laborious roles of nurse and mother, until finally the frail body had broken under its heavy burdens.

She spoke to the minister first about her concern for her family, and then talked about her own worsening condition.

"I haven't been able to attend church, preacher. It's so far away, and there's always so much to do. But I'm afraid I'm going to die, and I don't know what to tell Jesus when he asks me about not going to church."

The Bishop said he looked into the large, sunken eyes of the small girl, and then took her thin, calloused hands in his own, as he said, "You won't have to tell him anything, child. Just show him your hands. He'll understand."

(7)   *The Gospel According To You*

There is a Gospel according to Matthew; a Gospel according to Mark; a Gospel according to Luke; a Gospel according to John; and a Gospel according to *you.*
Charles Spurgeon wrote:

> *We may print religious literature and scatter it over the land till, like falling leaves, it drops at every man's door. But the world will not read books . . . it is too busy, too*

restless, too eager; but, my brethren, it will read you, and it will receive or reject the claims of religion of Christ in proportion as it finds in your everyday work, your everyday life, the record which you are making, the witness you are giving. Lamps do not talk but they shine. A lighthouse sounds no drum, it beats no gong, and yet far over the waters its friendly spark is seen by the mariner. So let your actions shine out your religion. Let the main sermon of your life be illustrated by all your conduct.

— *Selected*

(8) *Stanley and Livingstone*

Henry Stanley, the newspaperman who searched for, and found, David Livingstone, said of the great African explorer and missionary:

Had my soul been of brass, and my heart of tin, the powers of my head had surely compelled me to recognize the Spirit of goodness which manifested itself in him. Had there been anything of the Pharisee or hypocrite in him, I would have turned away a skeptic, but my everyday study of him in health and sickness, deepened my reverence and increased my esteem.

— *Selected*

(9) *Preaching As We Walk*

It is said that one day Saint Francis told his monks to go with him to the village where they would preach. The group left the monastery and went down through the village. They walked up and down the streets, stopping on numerous occasions to chat with the townspeople. Finally they walked back to the monastery. At the

14

gate one of the young monks boldly spoke up, "But you said we were going out to preach. When shall we begin?"

Francis answered:

My brothers, we have been preaching all the time we have been walking. We have been preaching in streets, market places, in shops. We have been observed, and our behavior was marked; and so we delivered a morning sermon for Christ. My sons, it is of no use that we walk anywhere to preach unless we preach as we walk.

— Selected

(10)   *Professor Schnozzlepozzle's Question*

The leading scientists of the world had worked on the giant computer for years. Every bit of conceivable data had been entered into the great wonder, and now the scientists were ready for the supreme test.

"What shall we ask it? What shall we ask it?" they all clamored.

"I know! I know!" exclaimed Professor Schnozzlepozzle. "We'll find out how the vast universe was created!"

"That's splendid! That's splendid!" shouted the others. "Ask it how the vast universe was created!"

And so Professor Schnozzlepozzle entered the great question very carefully: **HOW WAS THE VAST UNIVERSE CREATED?**

And the scientists held their breath as the huge machine whirred and whined, then flashed these words on the large screen:

SEE THE HOLY BIBLE: GENESIS, CHAPTER 1

(11)   **With Faith, Sometimes You Get Wet**

Three men of the cloth were fishing on a small lake. The Roman Catholic priest sat on one end of the long boat, the rabbi on the other end, and the Protestant minister in the middle. "I left my best lure in the cabin," said the priest. "I'll be right back." He then got out of the boat and, to the rabbi's astonishment, walked across the water to the shore.

"Wait on me," called the Protestant. "I think I'll get a cup of coffee." He then moved to the end of the boat, stepped out, and proceeded to walk toward shore.

The rabbi was utterly amazed, but finally, after due deliberation, decided that if his friends could walk on water, he could also. He then leaped out of the boat with great confidence, hit the water — and immediately began to sink.

When the Roman Catholic and the Protestant heard the splash, they looked around, saw the rabbi haul himself into the boat, and then, with great determination, jump out again only to disappear into the deep.

"We'd better get back," said the Roman Catholic, "and show him where those rocks are before he drowns himself."

(12)   **The Stubborn Bullsnake**

While driving near our home, I noticed a large bullsnake stretched lazily across the pavement. I stopped, picked the snake up, and took it to a safer environment nearby. Two days later, I was driving in the same area when I saw the snake once more sunning himself on the street. Again, I picked the stubborn fellow up and deposited him in a field far from the highway.

I have no idea what degree of intelligence bullsnakes possess, but I doubt that their I.Q.s rate very high in the reptile world. We, as human beings, however, cannot use ignorance as an excuse for our foolishness. The Scriptures state that we are created "a little lower than the angels," with the ability to discern between right and wrong, good and bad, and with the common sense to make the right choice. And yet, in spite of this great gift, it is often necessary for God to pause and to mercifully lift us from the dangerous situations in which we become involved.

We would doubtless be quite surprised if we knew just how often he *did* intervene on our behalf.

(13)   **"If Only That Horse Were a Member of My Church!"**

One day Henry Ward Beecher saw a horse he wanted to purchase. "This horse is sound," said the owner. "He is able to go any gait: walk, trot, pace, or gallop. He will work any place you put him, and he will neither bite nor kick. He will stand without hitching, is gentle, but full of spirit. He goes with only a nudge, in any direction you indicate, and he stops whenever you want."

"Ah," said Beecher, "if only that horse were a member of my church!"

(14)   **You Can't Take It With You!**

I was sitting in a barber shop one day when Mr. R—, a wealthy gentleman, well-known in the community, and owner of the building housing the barber shop, walked in and sat down in the next chair. The conversation varied, but soon got around to religion.

One of the barbers had recently become a Christian, and as Mr. R— started to leave, the barber invited him to attend church the following Sunday. "I would be happy to have you go with me and my family, Mr. R—," said the barber. "No, but I thank you," Mr. R— answered. "I am going out to look over some property I want to buy. Anyway, my stomach has been acting up a little, and any extra time I have, I'll spend in bed." Another barber spoke up, "Mr. R—, what are you going to do with all that money when you're gone? You can't take it with you, you know." Mr. R— laughed as he went out the door. "No, but I'll tell my wife to bring it with her when she comes!" The next week I was walking by Mr. R—'s home when I saw an ambulance parked in front. A few minutes later, Mr. R— was carried out on a stretcher, placed in the vehicle, and taken to a hospital where it was learned that he was suffering from cancer. A few days later he died.

The above is no condemnation of Mr. R—. He was my friend and a generous, kind man who contributed greatly to the community, but his casual attitude concerning the secular and the spiritual is similar to that held by most of us. We often forget that while the accumulation of material things may not be a sin in itself, it is easy to allow the quest for materialism to become the dominant force in our lives. When that happens, our Christian effectiveness is seriously diminished.

We should remember that we can neither "take it with us," nor expect someone else to "bring it along when they come."

18

(15)   **A Very Dry Sermon**

Chief Rain-In-The-Face was persuaded to attend a camp meeting. When it was all over, someone asked him what he thought of the speaker. "Ugh!" he grunted. "Big wind, lotta' dust, no rain."

— *Selected*

(16)   **The Old Iron Skillet**

I have an old iron skillet which through the years has accumulated a thick crust on the outside. Now I like this old skillet, crust and all, and one day when a friend told me how I might remove the crust, I was slightly indignant. "Remove the crust? Why, my skillet wouldn't be the same!"

After some thought, however, I decided that my friend was right. If I removed the crust, my skillet would serve me better, and it certainly would look better and feel lighter.

So it is with our lives. Perhaps we have accepted Christ and have tried to serve him, but over the years, with things left undone, prayers gone unprayed, unkind words spoken, and other wayward acts committed, we have allowed a hard crust to settle on our lives.

This crust can keep us from living our lives fully and completely for Christ and the church. Like the old iron skillet, we can be renewed and our burdens made lighter by changing our lives. Sometimes, a change is difficult because we are admitting that we have failed in many ways.

But Christ will understand, and once the crust is removed, it is certain that we will be much happier — and more effective in the work of the Kingdom.

— *Janet Morris*

(17)   **Long Distance**

Did you hear about the preacher who called another preacher long distance? It was a parson-to-parson call.

— Selected

(18)   **Lost Yesterday**

Horace Mann wrote:

Lost yesterday, somewhere between sunrise and sunset, two golden hours, each set with sixty diamond minutes. No reward is offered, for they are gone forever...

(19)   **The Clock**

In the city of Middlesboro, Kentucky, there is a large clock towering over the Montgomery Ward building in the center of town. For a very long time that clock has been a sentinel of time, sounding its warning chimes to those who might have tarried too long on their ways to work, to school, or to some special appointment. Many townspeople have depended upon that clock, and on the occasions when its accuracy would fail, some businesses might not open at the accustomed time, and many children would enter the nearby vine-covered schoolhouse long after the tardy bell had sounded.

Just as many depend on a clock and are influenced by it, so are they also dependent upon, and influenced by, the lives of others. Each person casts a shadow upon the world, and that shadow falls upon others every day with its passing always noted. An influence can be for good or for evil, but the presence of every person is noted by many others in the course of a lifetime.

(20)   **Following a Light**

Late one night, some years ago, I was driving on a winding, mountainous road in Eastern Tennessee when the headlights of my car suddenly went out. Fortunately, there was a car in front of me and I managed to stay on the road until I was eventually led to the foot of the mountain by following the car's rear lights.

That motorist never knew of my dependence upon him, but for a while, his life touched mine and I was the better for it.

(21)   **A Kind Word for Old Satan**

An elderly lady was noted in her village for her good nature, and especially for having a good word for everybody. One day, when someone in the village had been guilty of an especially mean action, all joined in the condemnation — except for the little woman with the sweet disposition. One of her gossipy neighbors was a little angry.

"Do you know, Mary, I believe you would have a good word for old Satan himself."

"Well," Mary replied, "he is a very industrious soul."

— *Selected*

(22)   **Strength In Weakness**

"My grace is sufficient for thee: for my strength is made perfect in weakness." (2 Corinthians 12:9)

During a long term of illness the above words

brought great comfort to me. Certainly they should be comforting to all, because they are words of Jesus, spoken to Paul, and applicable to those who are both physically ill and spiritually weak. Whatever our condition, whoever we are, and whatever we are, Jesus says to each of us, "My grace is sufficient for thee; for my strength is made perfect in weakness."

(23)   **Burma Buddhists**

Three laymen were sitting in a drugstore enjoying a coffee break when one of them brought up the subject of religion. "We have pretty good crowds at our services," he said, "but there doesn't seem to be any *real* interest."

"I know what you mean," said the second. "Our church attendance has been going downhill for a long time. Nobody seems to care except the elderly, and many of them aren't able to do anything."

"The trouble," said the third, "is that there are too many "Burma Buddhists" in the world."

"What do you mean?" asked the others. "What is a 'Burma Buddhist' "?

"Well," said the third, "the Buddhists of Burma have a saying that life is divided into three parts. The first part of life is for pleasure; the second part is for the accumulation of money and goods; and the third part is for religion. And that description seems to fit most of us perfectly."

(24)   **The "Unbreakable" Dishes**

The new "unbreakable" dishes were just being readied for the consumer market. As a student-salesman in the Southern area of Virginia, I accepted the job of helping to introduce the dishes to certain families in a kind of customer-reaction test. I called on a family one afternoon and began a long sales talk on the dishes' durability and ended by stating that they were absolutely unbreakable. To demonstrate, I tossed a plate on the tiled kitchen floor — and watched in red-faced embarrassment as it shattered into a half-dozen pieces.

Finally, I regained enough courage to look up into the laughing eyes of the man and woman. The husband broke the solemn silence, saying in a kind, patronizing tone, "That's all right, son, you needn't be embarrassed. We're used to exaggerated claims. You see, we have two politicians and one preacher in the family."

(25)   *Appearances May Be Deceiving*

There are few of us who do not often make snap judgments regarding others — usually based on first appearances. But appearances can be deceiving. When Abraham Lincoln was running for the Presidency, one newspaper editor cruelly condemned him because of his awkward bearing.

As a police officer, I usually found that appearances were seldom reliable. The most innocent of faces could harbor the cruelest and most evil minds. And of course, the reverse was true. The individual who looked most vicious was often kind and innocent.

It is dangerous — and wrong — to judge someone because of appearance. Only God can see into the heart, and, after all, that is what really counts.

(26)   **"As I Take a Look at You"**

They say God lives most everywhere, and I suppose that's true.
But oftentimes I wonder — as I take a look at you.
At you, the guy who creased my car at eighty-five miles per.
If you had stopped, I'd told you off, you crazy, speeding cur!

They say his Spirit touches all, and I suppose that's true.
But oftentimes I wonder, as I take a look at you.
At you — the clerk with scowling face, who short-changed me a dime.
Well, I'll get even, that's for sure, I'll short-change you next time!

They say Christ walks among us all, and I suppose that's true.
But oftentimes I wonder, as I take a look at you.
At you — who gives no kindness, love, as far as I can see.
What did you say? How dare you say, *it's all because of me!*

(27)   *Reminiscing*

When you are a youngster, it doesn't take much to excite you and bring happiness into your life. I remember the peace and contentment I enjoyed simply from lying on my side on the bank of the little stream that ran through the woods near our house. There I would watch the minnows as they darted about in the clear little pools, or wait for a bullfrog to climb up on a small island of moss.

And I can remember so well sitting in the kitchen eating a hot, buttered biscuit while I watched my mother moving busily about. Or perhaps I would gather my numerous cousins for a mountain-climbing expedition and scale the heights of the huge metal sign which towered invitingly over the highway, proclaiming boldly and colorfully:

RED GOOSE SHOES
Half the fun of having feet, Herbert Tamer's, 19th Street.

It didn't matter that we often came down from the sign much more quickly than we went up. It was all in the risks of mountain-climbing, and even with the cuts and bruises, we called it fun.

When one gets older, however, it sometimes seems to take a good deal more to bring contentment. The "little" things too often lose their appeal and we turn to more elaborate, involved, and sophisticated pleasures. Of course one cannot go about climbing signs in his middle-age, but one must admit that it would be safer than many of the other frenetic activities in which we sometimes become involved.

Sadly, the old joys may have passed from us, but the "little things" of our current life can often become big and wonderful things to us if we will but look around, consider the beauty and wonders of this great earth, and seek to enjoy them to the fullest.

(28)   ***Too Late — Too Late***

The darkness falls in sodden gloom, on gravestones worn by time and rain.

The wind against the weathered stones, crys out, "Too late-too late."

The lights have been, but now are gone; no more to see, to be.
Life's breath, with destiny of lives, has passed the boundary.

What did they do, where did they go? The wind bemoans their fate,
As, stirring over sunken mounds, it mourns, "Too late — too late."

They once were kings upon the earth, or peasants under rule. But now they sleep beneath the mouldering sod; a span of time is through.

What warning would they give us, as for other lives they wait?
They speak through wind-wails round the stones, "Don't wait, too late — too late."

(29)   **A Real Pane?**

A minister was called upon to substitute for another. The speaker began by explaining the meaning of the word "substitute."
"If you break a window and then place a piece of cardboard there, that's a substitute," he said.
After the sermon, the preacher was shaking hands with a woman who had listened intently to his message. Wishing to compliment him, she said, "Preacher, you were no substitute, you were a real pane!"

— *Selected*

(30) **Words of Wisdom**

Build A Better House: "Before you find fault with the house another has built, build another one."
Example: "The best example of man is yet but a poor imitation of Christ."
Forget It: "What is impossible to change is better to forget."
Temptation: "Some people seem to think that the only way to handle temptation is to yield to it."
Love: "He who has learned to really love is well on the way to the summit of Divine Perfection."
The Christian's Journey: "From *Penitence* to *Pardon* to *Power* to *Peace* to *Perfection.*"

— *Anonymous*

(31) **I Please My Friends**

A few preachers are like a few politicians. When pressed for their opinion on a controversial issue, they will answer in the following manner: "Well, some of my people are for it, and some of my people are against it.
"And I'm always solidly behind my people."

(32) **What Is Life To You?**

To a preacher life's a sermon, to the joker it's a jest; to the miser, life is money; to the loafer, life is rest. To the lawyer, life's a trial; to the poet, life's a song; to the doctor, life's a patient that needs treatment right along.
To the soldier, life's a battle; to the teacher, life's a school; life's a good thing to the grafter; it's a failure to the fool. To the man upon the engine, life's a long and heavy grade; it's a gamble to the gambler; to the merchant, life is trade.

Life is but a long vacation to the man who loves his work; life's an everlasting effort to shun duty, to the shirk; to the earnest, sincere worker, life's a story ever new; life is what we make it — brother, what is life to you?

— *S. E. Kiser*

(33)   **An Humble Prayer**

Give us not the power to rule — but the humility to serve. Let us not seek wisdom that we may be known of men — but rather let us seek wisdom that we may know God. Let us not walk in the darkness of the world, but in the light of heaven. Let us not seek to merely know Christ, but rather, let us strive, as Saint Paul, to become disciples of Christ.

(34)

A Preference for Light

A little girl was afraid of the dark and called for her mother. The mother sat on the bed and tried to comfort her.

"Don't be afraid," she said. "God is with you and will watch over you." The mother went out, thinking that the little girl would be consoled, but a few minutes later she heard the patter of little feet on the stairway and saw a small blonde head peek timidly over the stair rail.

"Mommy, if you don't mind, I'll let you sit with God and I'll stay down here in the light."

— *Selected*

(35)   **Faith Versus Reason**

"Faith, based on trust in God's infinite power is always more sensible than reason which depends upon our own limited faculties."

— *(Selected)*

(36)   **The Empty Tomb**

And behold, there was a great earthquake; for the angel of the Lord descended from heaven, and came and rolled back the stone. (Matthew 28:2)

. Of all the enemies that humanity must face, the most formidable obstacle seems to be death. George H. Boker, in his poem "Countess Laura" says, "I am that blessing which men fly from — Death."

While it is true that we attempt to fly from death, none, of course, are successful. Death is a certainty that each person must face at one time or another. Yet, death can be a blessing, although we seldom think of it in this respect. Death is an oasis of refuge and rest to the old, weary Christian. It is a blessed welcome to one who has "fought the fight and run the race," as Saint Paul did.

It is a symbol of attainment, reunion, and perfection to others. But to most, it remains a fearful journey into the valley of the shadows. That is because death often comes in sudden, violent ways, severing the ties of love in jagged agony. Death and the tomb are symbols of suffering, fear, and doubt.

But — thanks be to God! The empty tomb of Jesus is a symbol of victory, peace, hope — and eternal life!

(37)   **Brothers**

I am — You are — He is — A Child of God.
I am — You are — He is — We are — Brothers.

(38)   **The Battle of Life**

Fight, young friend, in life's swift race.
Fight to set the winner's pace!
Fight with courage, faith, and love.
Fight for halls of fame above!

(39)   **An Unnecessary Death**

In many respects, he was a genius. He could speak
five languages; discuss science, biology, or art with
ease and authority; and with his skillful hands, create
masterpieces from rough wood with a minimum of tools.

He had been associated with the rich, the powerful,
the educated, and the ordinary. He had traversed a large
area of the world. He was generous, kind, a great con-
versationalist, and he had a wife and children whom he
dearly loved.

And yet, he was lonely, depressed, and wanted to
die.

I had known John for two years and I was aware of
some of his feelings: that in spite of his many talents
and successes, he considered himself a failure, and that
for some distant reason, felt his family would be better
off without him.

One day he entered a hospital, and though he was
certainly ill, the doctor said there was no physical reason why he should be getting weaker day by day. But

I knew the reason: John had willed himself to die, and he didn't deny it. In spite of my pleas to him, and the constant love and attention from his family, John fell into a coma and finally gave up completely. I wish I could have convinced John how much he was needed and how much he was really loved, but I failed. How I could have succeeded, I don't know, but I do know that I have thought of my friend many, many times with great sadness. I have thought of our friendship, of course, and of the many wonderful conversations we had together; but I have also thought of his needless death and the loss to the world of so much talent. I think also about the precious times he has missed with his family, and of how much they have missed by his absence.

And I think of the decisions for life and death that each of us is able to make. We can't always avoid sickness, accident, or natural disaster, but we can, to a large extent, control our minds. By attitude and action, we can often will ourselves to live — as long and as meaningfully as possible — to fulfill God's purpose for our lives.

God's will is for us to live. Should not his will be ours?

(40)   *The Voice of God*

Have you ever listened, really listened?
Not to the sounds of a busy world; people walking,
    people talking, horns blowing, factories going,
    rushing, rushing, faster, faster.
Have you ever listened, really listened?
    To leaves talking, as the wind whispers through
    the trees, to rain falling against a tin roof,
    or against a window, or upon the dry earth.

Have you ever listened, really listened?
To a brook in the meadow, to a cricket in the
   night, to a bird singing in the dawn of a summer
   day, to a baby crying, a breeze sighing.
Have you ever listened, really listened,
   to the voice of God?

(41)   **By the Side of the Road**

   When I was a youngster I spent as much time as possible with my Aunt Mary and Uncle Harry, who lived in
a small house on a dirt road some distance from the city.
   I have numerous memories of that happy home
.tucked away, not only in my head, but also in my heart.
My aunt was a private nurse who helped others, not only
in her profession, but every day, at every opportunity.
Uncle Harry had been wounded in the First World War,
and when he walked, he leaned on a hand-carved cane.
But if his disability ever bothered him, he gave no indi-
cation of it in his relationships with others. I can remember walking with him for miles to a neighbor's house,
where he would give some assistance, often through
physical hardship, but always in a jovial manner.
   At other times, Uncle Harry and I would sit on the
small front porch, in the unique and comfortable slat-
ted, wooden chairs which he had made himself. Occasionally Uncle John, who lived nearby, would come over
and the conversation would turn to horses, or Uncle Tom
would come out from the city, and he would invariably
start kidding me about my interest in pretty twelve-year-
old Ann who lived down the road. And usually, before
we had talked for long, the arrival of neighbors — or
even strangers passing by — would necessitate the carrying out of more chairs, and the growing group would

expand out into the yard. There, the philosophies of life were discussed, and the problems of the world were solved.

With a glass of Aunt Mary's iced tea in one hand, and a biscuit sandwich made of homemade blackberry jam in the other, I listened and learned.

I don't remember much about the world problems of that day, but I do remember the basic values which I gained from those discussions. Aunt Mary and Uncle Harry believed in the basic goodness of people, and that belief was prominent in all those discussions. They certainly did not believe in strangers, because they never met any. I doubt that a person ever passed that house when they were outside, that they did not speak to, wave to, or invite in for food or conversation.

In their "little house by the side of the road," Aunt Mary and Uncle Harry lived a simple philosophy of neighborly love.

(42)   *"Gone Home"*

I was getting ready to leave for a convention in a distant state when I received the letter from Aunt Mary telling me of the serious illness of Uncle Harry. I changed my itinerary so that I would be able to stop and visit these beloved relatives. When I arrived at the little frame house, however, the ambulance was just leaving with the body of my uncle who had died shortly before.

As I rushed up on the familiar porch, my aunt met me with tears in her eyes, but a smile on her face. As she embraced me, she said simply, sadly, and yet joyfully, "Your Uncle Harry's gone home."

Even in the depths of sorrow, our burdens are made lighter when we remember that death — to those who love God — is only the beginning of a greater life.

(43)   *Our Greatest Need*

Religion is the supreme need of society in a world
that is disintegrating before our very eyes for lack of an
authority that shall be something more than force, for
lack of a spirit that shall be stronger than its fears and
hates and selfishness, and for lack of a faith that will
give meaning to life and courage to live.

— Harris Franklin Rall

(44)   *Rhyme and Reason*

The optimist fell ten stories. At each window bar he
shouted to his friends: "All right so far."

(45)   *The Stonecutter's Tribute*

It is said that this gravestone stands in a North
Carolina cemetery:

*Here lies Jane Smith, wife of Thomas Smith, marble
cutter.*
*This monument was erected by her husband as a trib-
ute to her memory and as a specimen of his work.*
Monuments of the same style, $350.00.

(46)   *From Dust To Dust*

A little boy attended the funeral of a neighbor with
his mother. He was much impressed by the words of
the preacher who said: "From dust you came and to dust
you go."
Before going to bed that night, the nervous young
fellow carefully locked his windows, checked his closet,
and then looked under the bed where he saw a small

34

pile of dust.

"Mama, Mama, come quick!" he cried. "Somebody's under my bed either coming or going!"

— *Selected*

(47)   **The Devil Made Her Say It**

A man had been invited to a costume party, and with meticulous care he made himself up as the devil, complete with horns. While driving to the party, his car broke down in front of a tent where a revival was being held. Seeking help, he entered the tent, but upon seeing him, the people scattered in all directions, thinking the devil had invaded their meeting. One lady tripped over a chair, and when the "devil" approached her, she quickly proclaimed: "Satan, I know this looks bad, but it's not what it seems. Even though I've been a church member for twenty years, I've been on your side all along!"

(48)   **To Forgive Is Not Impossible**

General Robert E. Lee was once asked by Jefferson Davis to give his opinion of a fellow officer who was being considered for an important position. Lee gave the officer an excellent recommendation and he was immediately promoted. Some of Lee's friends told him that the officer had said some very bitter things against him, and were surprised at the general's recommendation.

"I was not asked," said Lee, "for the officer's opinion of me, but for my opinion of him."

— *Selected*

(49) **An Active Faith**

A little farm girl was telling her friend about her brother, who placed rabbit traps in the fields around their home. "I prayed that God wouldn't let the little rabbits go into the traps, and he didn't, 'cause I kicked the mean old things to pieces."

(50) **The Destructive Nature of Man**

The sun and the moon and the stars would have disappeared long ago, had they been within reach of man.

— *Havelock Ellis*

The life of humanity upon this planet may yet come to an end, and a very terrible end. But I would have you notice that this end is threatened in our time not by anything that the universe may do to us, but only by what man may do to himself.

— *John Holmes*

(51) **Kindness**

When a bit of kindness hits ye, After passing of a
    cloud,
When a bit of laughter gets ye, An' yer spine is feel-
    ing proud,
Don't forget to up an' fling it, At a soul that's feel-
    ing wee,
For the moment that ye sling it, it's a boomerang to
    ye.

— *Captain Jack Crawford*

(52)   **The Grave a Thoroughfare**

When I go down to the grave I can say, like so many others, I have finished my work; but I cannot say I have finished my life; my day's work will begin the next morning. My tomb is not a blind alley; it is a thoroughfare. It closes in the twilight to open in the dawn.

— *Victor Hugo*

(53)   **No Sympathy Here**

Young man: Reverend Smith, your daughter has said she wants to become my wife.

Preacher: Well, don't come to me for sympathy. You might have known something would happen to you, hanging around the parsonage every night.

— *Selected*

(54)   **The Santa of Ward 17**

I was a very young man who had been lying for months in an Army hospital. Christmas was just weeks away and most of us in the ward were restless, lonely, and in some pain. President Truman had recently signed the bill which integrated the armed forces, and our hospital ward was expecting the transfer of several patients of other races. We had no idea, however, that one of these would turn out to be a November Santa Claus.

When the nurse wheeled him in, he certainly wasn't wearing a red suit, just the traditional green hospital pajamas. Neither did he have a white beard, although it would have contrasted nicely with his dark skin. And he obviously wasn't wearing a red hat, because it wouldn't have fit on his misshapen head. Much of the top of his head was gone, the skull caved in, and a steel plate covering his brain.

He was very much alive, however, even though he — as all of us — knew that his time on earth was severely limited. Yet this giant of a man did not dwell on death, and he was determined that the rest of the ward would also concentrate on life.

In spite of his suffering, he continually moved around the ward, laughing, telling jokes, trying to cheer the rest of us up. For weeks, he brought life and light to that gloomy hospital ward. And when he was gone, there was a great sadness at our loss. But the grief was tempered by our gratitude for the Christmas presents we had received: new hope, courage, and a valuable lesson in brotherhood; all from the "Santa of Ward 17."

(55)   **Some Things To Remember**

Condemning Fingers: When a man points a finger at someone else, he should remember that three of his fingers are pointing at himself.

— Selected

The Way You Live: He lived in eternity, which is a manner of living, not a length of life.

— Sir Walter Raleigh

God's Handwriting: Never lose an opportunity of seeing anything that is beautiful; for beauty is God's handwriting.

— Ralph Waldo Emerson

(56) **From Darkness To Dawn**

The *Super Chief* moved slowly through the Colorado countryside, the heavy rain falling in great torrents as the engineer looked into the darkness at the increasing water level building around the tracks. The passengers alternately peered through the windows as the lightning cast its reflection on the flooded plains and chatted with each other in attempts to ward off the growing apprehension within the cars.

The watch went on throughout the night as the thunder rolled and the rain continued to fall. The train had slowed to a crawl, but as the first light of dawn began to filter through the heavy clouds, the train began to increase its speed.

In one of the cars, a woman breathed an audible sigh of relief as she watched the increasing light of the new day. "Thank God for the morning," she said. "I never knew the light to look so good!"

(57) **To Love an Enemy**

A story is told of an event which occurred during the American Revolutionary War concerning Peter Miller, a Pennyslvania pastor of a small Baptist church.

Near the church lived a man who despised Miller and the Baptists, and who continually sought ways to abuse and persecute them. The man was also a traitor, and he was soon caught and sentenced to be executed. No sooner was the sentence pronounced than Peter Miller set out on foot to visit George Washington, at Philadelphia, to intercede for the man's life. He was told by Washington that the request for his friend could not be granted. "My friend!" exclaimed Miller. "I have not a worse enemy living than that man."

"Do you mean," said Washington, "that you have walked sixty miles to save the life of your enemy? That, in my judgment, puts the matter in a different light. I will grant you his pardon."

The pardon was made out and Miller at once proceeded, on foot, to a place fifteen miles distant, where the execution was to take place that same day. He arrived just as the man was being carried to the scaffold. Seeing Miller in the crowd, the condemned man remarked, "There is old Peter Miller. He has walked all this way to have his revenge by seeing me hanged."

But scarcely had he spoken when Miller presented the pardon, making his enemy a free man.

— Selected

(58)   ***Memories***

As I sit at my study window, I can hear the laughter of the children at play, and see them busily and happily playing the old familiar games, and trying to devise new ones from their own imaginations.

As I watch them, warm memories of my own youth are recalled. My children are content to dig a little hole in the New Mexico sand, filling it with water from the garden hose, and sailing little plastic boats from one shore to the other. I can remember the stream that ran through the woods near our home. My brother and I would dam up the stream, then go swimming in the clear, shallow water, or we would make a boat from an old washtub and paddle around pretending we were captains of a mighty ship.

The children now are hiding behind the clumps of alfalfa and tumbleweed, fighting for survival in the back yard, and I am reminded of the field of tall sage where, with my sister and cousins, we played as children. The sage waved as a mighty sea when the wind was blowing, and very vivid is the memory of the time I put flame to its windswept crests with a match I had sneaked from the top of the kitchen stove. The flames roared through the dry sage like a devouring lion while family and friends tried desperately to control its raging fury. The fire finally burned out with little damage, but considerable heat was placed on the seat of my pants.

I can now hear the church chimes in the distance, and as I listen, I recall the joy I experienced when I would be chosen to ring the church bell at the little, white frame church which I sometimes attended with Aunt Mary and Aunt Mattie. Nothing made me prouder than to tug on that frayed old rope, and usually I would become so immersed in my occupation that the pastor would have to stop me with a reminder that it was time for the first hymn.

Sadly, childhood does not last, and now I must be content to listen as I watch the children happily at play. But memories do last, and they grow fonder day by day.

And remembering the past can remind us that it is foolish to commit acts which foster bad memories when we have the capability for good. Memories of the wrongs we have committed can be unpleasant companions, but memories of the good things can be very comforting.

We should realize that the things we do today are the things we will remember tomorrow.

(59) **What Do You Know?**

A young minister had been asked to address a Sunday church school class on short notice. "Well, children, what shall we talk about?"

From the rear came a small voice: "What do you know?"

— *Selected*

(60) **Words To Ponder**

I am the resurrection and the life: he that believeth in me, though he were dead, yet shall he live: and whosoever liveth and believeth in me shall never die. Believest thou this?

— *John 11:25, 26*

Let not your heart be troubled: ye believe in God, believe also in me. In my Father's house are many mansions: if it were not so, I would have told you. And if I go and prepare a place for you, I will come again, and receive you unto myself; that where I am, there ye may be also.

— *John 14:1-3*

(61) **Victory**

I count him braver who overcomes his desires than him who conquers his enemies; for the hardest victory is the victory over self.

— *Pythagoras*

(62) **Yesterday — Today — Tomorrow**

There are two days in every week about which we should not worry, two days which should be kept free from fear and apprehension.

One of these days is *yesterday* with its mistakes and cares, its faults and blunders, its aches and pains. *Yesterday* has passed forever beyond our control. All the money in the world cannot bring back *Yesterday*. We cannot undo a single act we performed; we cannot erase a single word we said. *Yesterday* is gone.

The other day we should not worry about is *tomorrow,* with its possible adversaries, its burdens, its large promise, and poor performance. *Tomorrow* is also beyond our immediate control. *Tomorrow's* sun will rise, either in splendor or behind a mask of clouds, but it will rise. Until it does, we have no stake in *tomorrow,* for it is yet unborn.

This leaves only one day — *today.* Each of us can fight the battles of just one day. It is only when you and I add the burdens of those two awful eternities — *yesterday* and *tomorrow* — that we break down.

It is not the experience of *today* that drives us mad — it is remorse or bitterness for the things which happened *yesterday* and the dread of what *tomorrow* may bring.

Let us, therefore, live but one day at a time.

— *Selected*

(63)   ***Samaritans Are Not Onlookers***

A few years ago, while traveling a busy highway on Christmas Day, the car in front of me went out of control and overturned into a ditch. The occupants of the car were teen-aged boys, and one of them was thrown out and pinned under the automobile.

It wasn't long before three or four men were down in the ditch trying to lift the car off of the suffering youth. The task was difficult, however, and more help was needed. The curious had gathered along the bank, and in the crowd were several men, but it was some time before the pleas of the first rescuers persuaded some of the others to assist in lifting the vehicle.

The above true incident is illustrative of the compassion and concern most of us have for those in need, but it is also illustrative of the fact that there are many of us who are not so eager to cast our lot with the unfortunate. Lack of concern for those around us is a most frightful sin. Jesus answered the question, "Who is my neighbor?" by the story he told of the man who was beaten and robbed and left by the wayside. The priest and the Levite passed him by, but the Samaritan came to the injured one's aid. (Luke 10)

When a need exists, the person who is concerned does not hesitate, but seeks to fulfill that need. The dress of the person, the color of his skin, the religion he professes — or doesn't profess — are not important. What *is* important is that we, as individuals, must know that when we stop to help — either a neighbor or a stranger — we are fulfilling the primary responsibility which God has placed upon us.

(64)　　　　　　*The Wonders of God*

The naked eye can see approximately 6000 stars. With a powerful telescope many millions are visible. And there are billions of stars that remain unseen. The sun is 91 million miles from the earth, and the first fixed star about 19 billion miles away. The light we observe from this fixed star left its source 50,000 years ago.

But aside from all these wonders of God's magnificent creation, he is glorified by something even more astounding, more miraculous, more comforting — his perfect love as expressed through the redeeming grace of Jesus Christ.

A star is beautiful, but it gives no light into the blackness of a sin-darkened soul. The sun is a majestic and splendorous thing, but it offers no warmth to a broken body chilled by the fear of death. The atoms and molecules are as numerous as the moments of time it-self, and are filled with an unbelievable power, but the atoms can not offer the infinite power of redeeming love. The creation of the universe is an awesome miracle, but the creation reflects only a small bit of the total glory of the Creator.

To God be the glory, forever and forever!

— Selected

(65) *A Proposal Every Sunday*

"I understand your church is having small congre-gations," said one lady to another.

"Yes, so small that every time the preacher says, 'Dearly beloved,' you feel as if you had received a proposal."

— Selected

(66) *Alpha and Omega*

One day the Lord smiled down on Earth, and from this hallowed soil gave birth, to man, who fashioned from the sod, was mirrored by the soul of God. From this first day all time revolved, from this first human all evolved. Egypt, Africa, Caanan, Greece, everyone, with bonds of peace.

But from this mass of men and nations, hatred gushed with loud ovations. Again the Lord smiled down on Earth, and in a cave of virgin birth, came Jesus Christ, God's gift of love, to a dying world from realms above: Love thy neighbor, turn thy cheek, worship God, his Spirit seek. These words the Savior softly cried, and on the cross was crucified — killed by favor, fear, and hate, slain by all whose life's estate, consists of Hell's abominations, and the gutter's degradations.

Eden, Sodom, Holy City, sin abounded, gave no pity. Rome, Geneva, Auschwitz, Seoul, Dallas, Lebanon, Tupelo. Havana, Moscow, Satan boldly sows his chaff, reviles the holy. Philly, Birmingham, sin abounds, as from the throne God's love looks down; past color, class, and bounds of nation, into hearts of every station; pleading, seeking, right discerning, reserving hate for fires of burning; till one day he sailed again, sending Christ to rule and reign.

Over Adam, Moses, Paul, Wesley, King, Schweitzer, all — all who call upon his grace, looking up into his face, seeking help, their sins repent, to dwell in that eternal tent, where hate and evil have no home, but Truth and Love reign on the throne.

(67) **You Are Not Alone**

When you have shut your doors, and darkened your room, remember never to say that you are alone, for you are not alone; but God is within, and your genius is within — and what need have they of light to see what you are doing?

— *Epictetus,* Discourses, *14*

(68)

Gossip

Nothing is opened by mistake more often than the mouth.

A gossiper is like an old shoe whose tongue can never stay in place.

It is a good policy never to throw mud. Even though you miss your mark you'll still have dirty hands.

— *Selected*

(69) *A Little Girl's Prayers*

During the Second World War an American officer was staying with an English family during the London blitz. The constant bombing had played havoc with everyone's nerves, and faith seemed to be at its lowest point.

. Until one night when the officer overheard a member of the family — an eleven-year-old girl — praying:

O God, bless Mama, Daddy, Michael, Joan, Grandma, Captain Wilson, and all the people of London, and, O God, please take care of yourself or we'll all be sunk.

— *Selected*

(70) *Faith and Works*

An old Scotsman was operating a small rowboat for transporting passengers across one of the little lakes in Scotland. One day a passenger noticed that he had carved on one oar the word "Works," and on the other oar the word "Faith." Curiosity led him to ask the meaning of this. The old man replied, "I will show you," dropping one oar, and plying the other called "Works"; of course, they just went around in circles. Then he dropped that oar and began to ply the one called "Faith," and the little boat went around in circles again — this time in the opposite direction.

After this demonstration the old man picked up both "Faith" and "Works," and plying both oars together sped swiftly over the water, explaining to his inquiring passenger, "You see, that is the way it is in life as well as in the boat."

— *Canadian Churchman*

(71)   **Wanderers**

As a bird that wandereth from her nest, so is a man that wandereth from his place. (Proverbs 27:8)

Little birds sometimes get adventurous and leave their nests before Mother Bird is ready — and when they do, trouble often develops. So it is with man and his place in the pattern of life. A person's place is with God, and when one begins to wander or drift, one becomes like a bottle in an ocean current, or an automobile which slides out of control on an icy road.

It is easy to be deluded into thinking that we can always control our situations, but that is far from the truth. Each individual needs only to look back into his own life and he will realize that control under certain circumstances is almost impossible. Of course, we are responsible in the most part for the majority of these situations, and therefore are able to avoid much difficulty by avoiding such dangerous situations.

Avoidance of "danger zones" is easier than we would like to admit, but it does take faith, conviction, and perseverance. Swimmers usually find themselves in difficulty only when they get too far from shore, and boaters do not often get in much danger until they allow themselves to drift too far out onto the water.

Any time one allows oneself to drift away from God,

48

he or she is in great danger, but if we remember our place and stay within it, we need never worry.

And, thanks be to God, when we find that we have drifted too far away from our Father and Creator, we need only to cry out and he will hear our plea.

(72)   **To The Skeptic**

It is natural for every person to possess and exert a certain amount of skepticism concerning most things, even those things that are spiritual; but it is difficult to understand why a mature adult can accept so many wonders of life so matter-of-factly, yet still have doubts concerning the presence and power of Christ. After all, in our entire history there is no book which has had the lasting and influencing power of the Bible. And there has never been a person whose philosophy has touched so realistically and deeply such vast numbers of people as has that of our Lord. And there has never lived, in all the history of the world, a person who has spoken such wisdom, lived so perfectly, loved so nobly, and done such great works.

But most of all, there has never been one before who was so truly and gloriously resurrected from the bonds and darkness of death.

Can anyone *really* have doubts about Christ?

(73)   **The Casting of the Net**

How many times have you moved up and down the blue-green waters of a river, casting your line time and time again into the depths only to pull it in empty? But, just as you were about to give up, you cast your line into one last favorable-looking spot, and reeled in a surprisingly large fish.

It all depends upon where you cast the line.

The disciples had been fishing all night (John 21), yet they had caught nothing. They were casting on the wrong side. But when they heeded the voice of the Master and cast their net on the right side, they received a great abundance.

So can we all — if we cast our nets on the right side.

(74)   *The Greatest Commandment*

Thou shalt love the lord thy God with all thy heart, and with all thy soul, and with all thy mind, and with all thy strength. (Luke 10)

Heart: the "Union Station" of the body. *Soul:* the invisible, yet real and eternal, part of a person which keeps the body erect, moving, breathing, feeling, and living. *Mind:* our intelligence, common sense, conscience, and faculty for spiritual reception. *Strength:* the ability to fulfill the responsibilities of the above gifts.

— Selected

(75)   *The Touch of the Master's Hand*

It was battered and scarred and the auctioneer
Thought it scarcely worth his while
To waste much time on the old violin,
But held it with a smile;
"What am I bidden, good folks," he cried;
"Who'll start the bidding for me?
A dollar, a dollar, now two, only two,
Two dollars. Who'll make it three?"

Three dollars once, three dollars twice,
Going for three, but no;
From the back of the room a gray-haired man
Came forward and picked up the bow.
Then wiping the dust from the old violin
And tightening all the strings,
He played a melody pure and sweet,
As sweet as the angels sing.

The music ceased and the auctioneer
With a voice that was quiet and low,
Said, "What am I bid for the old violin?"
And he held it up with the bow.
"A thousand dollars, and who'll make it two?
Two thousand, and who'll make it three?
Three thousand once, three thousand twice,
And going, and gone," said he.

The people cheered, but some of them cried,
"We do not quite understand —
What changed the worth?"
Swift came the reply:
"The touch of the Master's hand."
And many a man with life out of tune,
And battered and torn with sin,
Is auctioned cheap to a thoughtless crowd
Much like the old violin.

A mess of pottage, a glass of wine,
A game and he travels on.
He is going once, he is going twice,
He's going, he's almost gone.
But the Master comes and the foolish crowd
Never quite understand
The worth of a soul and the change that is wrought
By the touch of the Master's hand.

— *Author Unknown*

(76)   ***Never Alone***

"I never once felt that I was alone. I always felt that God was there. And because of His presence, I felt in contact with all other men and women, everywhere."

— *Martin Niemoller*

(77)   ***"Hit Me Again!"***

An active church steward was invited to speak before a civic club but had been warned to limit his speech to thirty minutes.

At the end of an hour, he was still going strong and the master of ceremonies tried desperately to stop him by various hand signals, but the speaker merely ignored him.

Finally, in desperation, the emcee picked up the gavel, aimed and fired, but missed the speaker and hit a man in the first row. The man slumped forward, then groaned, "Hit me again, I can still hear him."

— *Selected*

(78)   ***Sayings To Remember***

On Going To Church: Merely going to church no more makes one a Christian than going to the bank makes one rich.

— *Roy McClain*

Getting Acquainted: If one is to love his neighbor as himself, the first step is to get acquainted with him.

— *Anonymous*

Longevity: People who live one day at a time usually live a long time.

— *Anonymous*

(79)   **Gossiping Preacher**

Four preachers met for a friendly gathering. During the conversation one preacher said, "Our people come to us and pour out their hearts, confessing their sins and needs. Let's do the same. Confession is good for the soul."

One minister then confessed that he was a movie fan and would sneak away to movies on occasion — sometimes to the naughty ones, too.

The second confessed to his liking for strong cigars and was not averse to ordering those smuggled in from Cuba. The third one confessed to playing cards, and sometimes lost quite a bit of money.

When they came to the fourth man, he wouldn't confess. The others pressed him, saying, "Come now, we confessed ours. What is your secret vice?"

Finally he answered, "It is gossiping and I can hardly wait to get out of here!"

— *Selected*

(80)   **Gratitude**

I was sorry I had no shoes, until I saw someone who had no feet.

— *Selected*

(81)   **God Remembers**

Every kindly word that's spoken,

Every vow that is not broken;
Every smile that tends to bless
A precious soul that's in distress,
God remembers.

Every deed however small,
Rendered kindly to a soul;
Every salty tear that's shed,
Every prayer that's humbly said,
God remembers.

All evil deeds He will forget,
If sincerely we repent;
But all things that we can claim
To have done in Jesus' name,
God remembers.

— *Edith Cawood*

(82)   ***Denominations***

Recently, as an excuse for not attending church, a fellow told me that he did not believe in church denominations, and he proceeded to elaborate upon the sins prevalent within denominationalism. This man's opinion of religious groups is not unique — in fact it is a very popular way of thinking, even among the various denominations themselves. Some groups spend more time and money expounding upon their own self-righteousness, trying to validate their own reasons for existence, and attempting to convert the members of the neighboring church than they do in reaching out with the Gospel of love.

This is not to say, of course, that all denominations are right or even justified in their existence, but before one condemns, it would be wise to remember that few of us are capable of passing judgment upon another. Denominationalism often provides numerous ways for human beings to commit wrongs and make errors, but it more often enables complex societies of people to worship and serve. Paul and Peter differed, but they worked together for the ultimate purpose. When John complained to Jesus about the follower of Christ who went his own way, Jesus answered, "He that is not against us is with us . . ." (Mark 9)

There is an old saying which goes:

There is so much bad in the best of us, and so much good in the worst of us, that it hardly behooves any of us to speak any ill of the rest of us.

There is another saying also worthy of consideration:

We may not be agreeable concerning many things, but we will never be disagreeable concerning Christly things.

(83)   The Great and the Small

I long to accomplish a great and noble task, but it is my chief duty to accomplish humble tasks as though they were great and noble. The world is moved along, not only by the mighty shoves of its heroes, but also by the aggregate of the tiny pushes of each honest worker.

— *Helen Keller*

(84)   *Names To Remember*

In past generations names have had more sig-
nificance and have assumed more importance than they
do in the present. This is particularly true concerning
the names of individuals, but the names of places also
provide some interest — and humor.

In the central area of Kentucky — which itself means
"land of tomorrow" or "dark and bloody ground" —
there are four communities within just a few miles of
each other called respectively, "Salt Lick," "Blue Lick,"
"Paint Lick," and "Red Lick." Further east in the same
state you will find towns with names like "Sand Gap"
(which town literally sits on a huge sand dune); "Para-
dise" (which sounds like a nice place to live); "Hot Spot"
(which doesn't sound so nice); and "Blacksnake" (which
sounds rather slinky).

In Arizona there is "Sunnyslope," in California
"Needles," in New Mexico, "Rattlesnake," and "Gila,"
and in West Virginia, places like "Three Churches,"
"Romance," "Christian," and 'Mud."

Pennsylvania boasts such place names as "Cuddy,"
"Crucible," "Forty Foot," "Gabby Heights," "Inter-
course," and "Plum."

The above names are interesting, and are obviously
intended in many cases to be descriptions of the respec-
tive towns. Names of individuals are also given for
descriptive purposes, as the Bible so clearly illustrates.

There is "Adam" which means "first man" or "father
of all living"; and "Eve" meaning "first woman" or
"mother of all living"; "Abraham," "father of nations," and
"Samuel" who was "asked of God" by his mother Hannah. In the New Testament we meet "Peter" the "rock,"
who, with his fellow-missionary, "Paul" the "worker"

(formerly known as "Saul" the "destroyer") helped to spread the "Gospel" or "good news" throughout the world.

But of all names, the most important by far is the name of "Christian." This name means many things to many people, but it indicates that one is a follower of Jesus Christ, the Son of God and Savior of the world. It is a name to be taken seriously, carried proudly — yet with humility — and used honestly, diligently, and reverently.

(85)   *Cities Without Christ*

Many ministers might agree that those who are most neglectful of the church are usually the ones who would make the loudest noise if the church were suddenly removed from their community; because even the agnostics want the steadying influence of the church around them.

All people would probably give more consideration to the church if they would pause for a moment and try to imagine their community without it. Aside from the church building, other structures which might be absent in a "heathen" community are the hospital, the children's homes, homes for the aged, the welfare agencies, many clubs and organizations, and possibly even the public libraries and schools. And, surprisingly to many, even the police and fire departments might be absent, since these institutions are related to Christian principles of brotherhood, equality, and concern for one's neighbor.

There are many more "side-effects" and "fringe benefits" of the Christian faith, but its more important purpose is to direct and motiviate the hearts and minds of humankind into a better, nobler, and more fruitful way of living.

Rather than try wilfully, or through neglect, to take the church out of the community, we should give ourselves completely to the joyous task of building and promoting the church — so that all people might come under its redeeming influence.

(86)   **The Accounts of God**

A farmer once wrote to an editor: .

Dear Sir:
I have been trying an experiment. I have a field of corn which I ploughed on Sunday. I planted it on Sunday. I cut and hauled it to the barn on Sunday. And I find that I have more corn to the acre than has been gathered by any of my neighbors this October.

The writer sent his letter, sure that the Christian editor could have no answer to the sneer implied in it. But imagine his feelings when in the next issue of the paper he read his own letter in print, and at the end of it this one sentence: "God does not make full settlement in October."

— Selected

(87)   **Eternal Life**

When we wonder how it is possible for us to live forever, we should also wonder how it is possible for us to live at all.

(88)   **Trust In God**

Trust with a child-like dependence upon God, and you shall fear no evil; for be assured that even "if the enemy comes in like a flood, the Spirit of the Lord will lift up a standard against him." While, at that dread hour when the world cannot help you, when all the powers of nature are in vain, when your heart and your flesh shall fail you, you will be enabled still to rely with peace upon Him who has said, "I will be the strength of thy heart and thy portion forever."

— *H. Blunt*

(89)   **Feuding Church Members**

Some years ago I was called upon to become a peacemaker for two elderly Sunday church school teachers who had been verbally "feuding" for years. Because of some long-forgotten disagreement, their only words to each other were comments of sarcasm and bitterness. Eventually they were reconciled, but not before they had done great damage to the mission of the church.

Of all the commandments to follow, the most difficult ones seem to be those which admonish us to "love our neighbor" and to "forgive those who trespass against us." And yet, we continue to call ourselves by the name "Christian."

(90)   **This Sunday, You Owe Me!**

The minister of a small church believed some practical joker was joshing him as I.O.U.s began to appear in the collection plate. But one Sunday night weeks later the collection included an envelope equal to the total of the I.O.U.s.

After that, the parson could hardly wait to see what amount the anonymous donor had promised. The range in contributions was from five to fifteen dollars — apparently based on what the donor thought the sermon was worth — for there came a Sunday when the collection plate brought a note reading, "U.O.Me $5."

— *Selected*

(91)   ***The Tax Man Visits***

An income tax inspector visited a clergyman and expressed a desire to see the church. The minister beamed with pleasure at the request. Afterwards he asked the inspector what he thought of it.

"Frankly, I'm a bit disappointed," said the government man. "After looking at the income tax returns of your parishioners and the fine gifts they claim to your church, I had come to the conclusion that the aisles must be paved with gold."

— *Selected*

(92)   ***Watermelon Seeds***

On a Sunday morning in 1969, the worshipers at Duke University Chapel emerged from the gothic sanctuary to find the church steps blocked by a few slovenly dressed young men and women sitting amid an abundance of broken watermelon pieces. The worshipers weaved down the steps and through the scattered garbage as the religious dissenters calmly continued their feast, their mindless purpose lost amid the ridiculous and somewhat comical picture which they presented. Many angry comments were made on both sides, but the classic statement came from an old man who gazed *upon the scene with the eyes of amused wisdom.*

It's not likely that a few young ruffians will destroy Christianity with a watermelon feast on the church steps, and who knows, it might even help some of us who have become so complacent and self-righteous if we slipped on a few watermelon seeds occasionally.

(93)   **Ouch**

A little boy was having a tooth filled. "Why are you yelling?" asked the dentist, "I'm a painless dentist." "Maybe you are," yelled the boy, "but I'm not!"

— *Selected*

(94)   **What Is**

A Phylactery? Mentioned in Matthew 23:5, these are strips of leather to which is attached a strong, square black box made of parchment, containing parts of the Mosaic Law from Deuteronomy. Two phylacteries are worn, one for the head and one for the arm. These are supposed to indicate devotion to the Lord.

(95)   **Going Down?**

In England in the 1960s, a minister was directing a church choir when the floor gave way and he fell several feet into a hole. The hymn being sung was, "I Cannot Help But Wonder Where I'm Bound."

Do you think somebody was trying to tell him something?

(96) **Going Down, 2**

Something to think about: Of the three and a half billion people in the world, Christians and Jews number about one fourth. Is somebody trying to tell us something?

(97) **Find Strength With God**

We cannot walk each day the same forever,
    So oft the ties we hold so true, must sever:
And yet, within His love we must abide,
    Lest for our faltering ways, He chides.

God knows our strength and our endeavor,
    Our failures, fears, and questions ever:
Someday, we know not when or where will be,
    The veil will be lifted and His face we'll see!

So if your cross at times is hard to bear,
    Just look about you, there are those who care:
Lift up your cross, lift up your face, and ever onward
    trod
    There is an unsurpassing strength,
    For those who walk with God!

— *Gertrude Howard*

(98)   *Of Church Worship*

To be of no church is dangerous. Religion, of which the rewards are distant, and which is animated only by Faith and Hope, will glide by degrees out of the mind, unless it be invigorated and reimpressed by external ordinances, by stated calls of worship, and the salutary influence of example.

— *Samuel Johnson*

(99)   *Worship Only God*

In 1960, I watched in amazement as great crowds of people fell to their knees in adoration, or stood weeping with joy, their arms outstretched, as Fidel Castro gave one of his long and emotional speeches in Havana Square.

In 1961, back in the United States, I received a letter from a Cuban friend who wrote me from New York after he fled his homeland to protect his family and his faith from the insidious corruption of Communism.

"We were deceived, all of us," he wrote. "When we found out the truth, it was too late. The situation is bad . . . there are many Russians in Cuba. Only the priests and ministers who submit to the teachings of Communism will be allowed any freedom. The government has taken the schools. I left everything, and today I registered as a refugee. Pray for us . . ."

Adoration does not belong to human beings — only to God. Even Jesus came as a suffering servant, to minister to humankind, and to give his life for all people. When we put our faith in humanity, we can only be disappointed. When our faith is in God, we are eternally secure.

(100)   **The Face of Christ**

Charles Lamb, looking at Robert Haydon's huge canvas on which Haydon painted *The Triumphal Entry Into Jerusalem* made a comment which is memorable. He said, "The face of Jesus looks remarkably like Haydon."

How often do we portray Christ as we are, not as *Christ* is!

— *Selected*

(101)   **A Strange Proposal**

A story is told of a shy country boy who had courted a girl for a long time, but could never find the right words to ask her to marry him. Once they were walking hand in hand in the cemetery, and as they passed the family plot of the country boy's clan, the right words finally came.

"How — how would you — like to be buried over there with my people?"

— *Selected*

(102)   **He Cared**

A different kind of "shy person" is that of Big John, who, in all of his seventy-eight years had never spoken a complete sentence, but who was paid the greatest tribute by a neighbor whose wife had recently died:

You know, I was mighty grateful to the preacher and all the neighbors who came around. They brought food, talked to me about God's will, and getting on with my life, and how things could get better by and by. I'm really thankful I got ·

such good friends. But you know, it was Big John that I guess I appreciated more than anybody. He never said a word, but he stayed with me through the hardest times, the rough times when all I could do was sit an' cry. And you know something? Big John just sat and cried with me! I know he really cared.

(103)   He Got the "Call"

A man attended a revival meeting in which the evangelist preached about the call of God leading men into ministry. At the end of the sermon the evangelist pointed his finger into the crowd and yelled out over and over, "Who will he send from this group? Who will go? Will it be *you? Will it be you? Who? Who will be called?*"

That night, the man got into bed, the preacher's words still echoing in his ears. And then, just as he was beginning to doze off, he heard a voice coming through his window, *"Who? Who?"*

The man bolted out of bed, grabbed his clothes, and ran out of the house, determined to find the evangelist and enlist at once in the army of God. Just as he stepped out the front door, he tripped, fell on his back and found himself looking up at a tree, directly into the eyes of an owl that called out loudly, "Who? Who? Who?"

(104)   God's Presence

There are times when I don't feel God's presence, but that may be the time when he's testing me most. That's when I walk by sheer faith.

— *Billy Graham*

(105) **A Pretty Picture**

A teenager rushed into a drugstore. "The preacher slipped from a ladder and he's hanging by his pants!" he gasped.

"My goodness!" said the druggist. "What can I do?"

"Hurry and put some film in my camera! He won't hang on for long!"

(106) **Communication Is Important**

A devout woman was talking to a neighbor. "I suppose I must go into the house and have my devotions," she said.

"Well, you certainly don't seem very cheerful about it, Agatha; what is wrong?"

"It's just that I'm sure God thinks I'm dead," the woman sadly replied.

"Why on earth would he think you were dead?"

"Because I haven't said my prayers for a whole week!"

(107) **Narrow-Minded Noise Makers**

Alexander Pope, referring to trouble-makers and narrow-minded people, wrote, "These people are like narrow-necked bottles — the less they have in them, the more noise they make in pouring it out."

(108) **Turn Loose!**

A little girl dropped a penny in an expensive vase, reached in to get it, and could not get her hand out. Her parents tried to free her, but couldn't. They called a doctor who was unable to help, and the only alternative left was the one they had tried to avoid.

"I suppose we're going to have to break the vase," said the father, "but let us try just one more time. Now I'm going to hold onto the vase again, dear, and I want you to relax your hand as much as you can while you pull."

"But daddy," said the little girl, in all childhood innocence, "if I relax my hand, I'll drop the penny I'm holding."

(109)   *A Reason Not To Evangelize*

In a small Oklahoma town, oil was struck on church land. The church had a congregational meeting to decide what to do with the rich proceeds from the oil. They voted to pay off church debts, make some needed improvements to the church building, put a small nest egg in the bank, and then divide the remainder among the church members. As soon as the latter decision was made, one of the members jumped up in the back and yelled, "I make a motion that we don't take in any new members!"

— Selected

(110)   *The Rest of the Story*

A little boy was looking in a religious store window at a picture of the crucifixion of Christ. A man stopped and also looked. "That's Jesus, mister," the little boy offered. "Wicked men killed him, and good men are going to bury him. I learned that in Sunday school."

"That's right, son," said the man, and he turned to walk away.

"Mister, mister! I forgot to tell you," yelled the little boy, "he rose from the dead and is now alive forever!"

— *Selected*

(111)   ***A Rough Job***

A couple had been married for a short time. The day after the honeymoon, the wife came home from work and cheerfully asked her husband what he had been doing all day.

"Filling the salt and pepper shakers," he said in a tired voice.

"Now don't tell me that took all day," she said laughingly.

"It certainly did!" he answered a littl defensively. "It isn't easy getting the salt and pepper through those little holes!"

(112)   ***Real Religion***

A small country church was having a revival meeting, and the evangelist called for confessions. One man was eager:

> *Brothers and sisters, you know I ain't been what I ought to of been. I've stole hogs and told lies and got drunk and cursed, but I thank the Lord there's one thing I ain't never done. I ain't never lost my religion!*

(113)   ***The Wrong Symbolism***

A man told this story of a shipwreck which occurred

while he was a sailor in the Nineteenth Century:

> *After being washed up on the island, I crawled for days through the wilderness, thinking any time I might be discovered by savages and killed, but finally I came to the top of a hill, looked down into a clearing, and saw a small village with a gallows built in the center. "Thank God," I said to myself, "I'm in a Christian land."*

(114)   *Think of the Future*

A gambler was converted during a revival and the preacher began to advise him. "The first thing you've got to do is to burn all your gambling equipment."

"But, preacher," said the gambler, "suppose I backslide. Then I'd be in a fine predicament!"

(115)   *Ignorance Is No Virtue*

A college professor was visiting some friends and attended a small church service with them. He was very upset when the untrained preacher focused in on the visiting professor as a target in a sermon against formal education. After the service, the professor went up to the preacher and said, "I understood you to brag about your ignorance from the pulpit. I just wanted to say that you have much for which to be thankful!"

— *Selected*

(116)   *A Short Sermon*

A young preacher just out of seminary asked an older one for advice. "Don't tell them what you don't know.

That will take too long. Just tell them what you know. That should make a good ten-minute sermon."

— Selected

(117)   *Not So Wonderful*

A teacher was speaking to her Sunday church school class about the wonders of the universe. "Isn't it marvelous to think that the light of the sun and the stars travels thousands of miles per second to reach the earth?"

"Not much," said a little boy. "It's downhill all the way."

— Selected

(118)   *Star of Wonder*

An awesome thought: If you traveled in a spacecraft at the speed of 25,000 miles an hour, it would take you almost 115,000 years to reach Earth's nearest star (other than the sun). And this is just one of God's innumerable wonders!

(119)   *Change Comes Hard — If At All*

"One should think," said a friend to Dr. Samuel Johnson, "that sickness and the view of death would make men more religious."

Sir, they do not know how to go to work about it. A man who has never had religion before no more grows religious when he's sick than a man who have never learned figures, can count when he has need of calculation.

(120) Noise Isn't Necessary

An elderly woman, visiting a church for the first time was somewhat disturbed by the loud preaching of the young minister. At the end of the service, he stood at the door shaking hands. The woman passed by, took his hand firmly and looked him right in the eye. "Young man," she whispered, "if you moved closer to the Lord, you wouldn't have to yell!"

(121) Keeping Watch

It was very late and the good bishop had been sitting at his desk for hours, worrying about his many church problems. Suddenly, a still, small voice spoke gently from the apparent emptiness. "Bishop," it said, "this is the Father. You can go to bed, now. I'll sit up for the rest of the night."

(122) The Presence of the King

The telephone rang one morning in a Washington church. "Do you expect the president to attend church this Sunday?" the voice inquired. "That I cannot promise," answered the pastor, but we do expect the Lord to be here and that should be incentive enough for a good attendance. Will you join us?"

— *Selected*

(123)   **A Lazy Faith**

"Hey!" shouted the passing motorist. "Your house is on fire!"
"I know it, stranger," nodded the mountaineer.
"Then why aren't you doing something about it?"
"I am. I'm praying for rain."

(124)   **Too Easy?**

In a store window there was an exhibit of many kinds of crosses. Underneath was a sign which read:
Easy Terms

(125)   **Footprints**

Remember that the footprints in the sands of time were not made by someone who was sitting still doing nothing.
— *Author Unknown*

(126)   **Just A Step Away**

They who love are but one step away from heaven.
— *James Lowell*

(127)   **Jim's Faith**

An atheistic master once belittled the Christian faith of one of his slaves. "Jim," he said, "you are the biggest fool I ever knew. You are always talking about faith

72

in God. I suppose you think that if the Lord should tell you to jump through a stone wall, your faith would take you through."

"Master," said the slave, "if the Lord tells Jim to jump through that stone wall, it's Jim's business to jump, and the Lord's business to get Jim through."

(128)　　　　**A Perceptive Child**

A little boy said to his father one day, "Daddy, when you stand up to preach, I always say a prayer."

The father glowed at the thought that his son prayed for him every time he preached. "What prayer do you say for Daddy, Son?"

"When you stand up to preach I always pray, 'Now I lay me down to sleep.' "

(129)　　　　**Tomorrow**

"Don't put off till tomorrow what you can do today, because today was yesterday's tomorrow."

(130)　　　　**Domine Quo Vadis?**

In the city of Rome is a small church called *Domine Quo Vadis.* The words are Latin and mean, "Lord, whither goest Thou?"

It is said that in A.D. sixty-five as Peter awaited his death in prison, he was overcome with fear and managed to escape. As he ran from the city, at the spot where the church now stands, he met Christ himself. Amazed at the sight of his Savior, he asked, "Lord, whither goest Thou?"

The sad voice of Jesus answered, "Peter, I go to Rome to be crucified anew in your place." At once Peter's courage returned and he turned back — to face the cross.

— *Selected*

(131)   **Real Devotion**

Outside the cemetery of Greyfriars Churchyard in Edinburgh stands a monument erected to the memory of a dog named Bobby. Bobby's master died and was buried in the cemetery. Bobby came to the funeral and refused to leave the grave. As the months passed, townspeople fed the dog and occasionally took him into their homes, but Bobby always went back to the grave. After four years, the hardship of the weather and his own grief finally overcame the faithful dog. He died, lying on his master's grave, ever faithful to the end.

(132)   **Mr. Smith's Overcoat**

A timid minister was in a restaurant eating, when he noticed a man get an overcoat off a wall hanger and begin to put it on. The timid minister walked up and gently touched the man on the arm. "Excuse me," he said very quietly, "but do you happen to be Reverend Smith of Lexington?"

"No, I'm not!" the man answered impatiently.

"Oh — er — well," stammered the timid preacher, "you see, I am, and that's his overcoat you're putting on."

74

(133)   *The Righteous and The Unrighteous*

Once upon a time, two men met in a church, looked at each other coldly and then smiled and said, "Hello." The first prayed later:

> God, I thank thee that I am not like him. He comes to church, but he cheats on his wife and his income tax as well. Since the church is full of hypocrites like him, I'm glad that the only thing that brings me to this place is the baptism of my grandchild.

The second prayed:

> God, I thank thee I can come here each week and give generously, and that I can go regularly to the Sacrament, and that you have not made me like this hypocrite who comes to your house only because his grandchild is being baptized.

Behind the two men sat two women. The first woman prayed thus:

> Lord, I love everyone around me so much, but I am angry with you, for you have not answered my prayers as I think you ought, and you are not running the world the way I want it run.

The second woman said:

> Lord, I love you, but I can't see why you let all those others get away with their hypocrisy. They do not come here out of the pure motives that I have.

In other places in the church, prayers were ascending that contained many phrases and thoughts. "Why is the organ so loud?" "Why do they pick hymns I don't know?" "Why is he preaching today?" "It's too hot in here." "I wonder if I turned the microwave on with the roast?" "We have to stand too much." "I can't sing when I'm sitting down."

And God smiled and said:

It is well that it is Sunday, and that these people have gathered in this place, for if ever there were people who need to be in my presence and in the presence of each other, it is these.

— *A. Hermeier,* Lutheran Standard

(134)   *A Fast Talker*

A teenager went into an ice cream shop, bought a soda, gulped it down, slapped a half dollar on the counter and left. The soda jerk slipped the coin into his pocket, noted that the owner saw him and came up with a fast answer.

"What a crazy kid," he said nonchalantly, "he comes in, leaves a half dollar tip, and walks out without paying!"

(135)   *Another Fast Talker*

A man with a prison record was caught crawling through a broken window of a church. He explained to the police, "I was just looking for a place to pray."

(136)   *The Easy Way*

The trouble with people these days is that they want to reach the promised land without going through the wilderness.

— *Selected*

(137)   **The Vision of Luther**

Martin Luther once said that during a severe illness, he seemed to see Satan coming toward him with a large scroll on which were listed all the sins of his life. The triumphant devil unrolled it before him saying, "These are your sins. There is no hope of your going to heaven." Luther read the long list with growing consternation when suddenly he realized that there was one thing not written there. "The list is true," he said, "but one thing you have forgotten, and that is, the blood of Jesus Christ cleanseth from all sins."

— *Selected*

(138)   *Erasures*

A distraught man insisted that he had given a signal before his car was struck by another. "Look, mister," said the investigating policeman, "I was standing on the corner and saw the entire incident. Your arm went up and down, and then around in circles!"

"My goodness!" exclaimed the man, "The first two signals were wrong! Didn't you see me trying to erase them?"

(139)   *A Rare Sight*

Few people know the name of George Matheson, but millions have sung a hymn he wrote. Matheson was a brilliant scholar with a promising career, but he suddenly lost his sight. It did not prevent him, however, from writing these memorable words:

O light that followest all my way, I yield my flickering torch to Thee;
My heart restores its borrowed ray, That in Thy sunshine's glow its day,
May brighter, fairer be.

O Joy, that seekest me through pain, I cannot close my heart to Thee;
I trace the rainbow through the rain, And feel the promise is not vain,
That morn shall tearless be.
— *"O Love That Wilt Not Let me Go"*

(140) Speak Kindly

Have a good word for everybody. The only person who has a right to look down on another is one in an airplane. Even the tombstones speak well of those beneath them.

— *J. H Turner*

(141) Sign at the Bottom

A woman once asked a minister what his idea of consecration was. The pastor took a blank piece of paper and held it before the woman. "Consecration is to sign your name at the bottom of this blank sheet of paper and let God fill it in as he wills."

— *Selected*

78

(142)   The Real Riches

Let me hold lightly things of this earth;
Transient treasures, what are they worth?
Moths can corrupt them, rust can decay;
All their bright beauty fades in a day.
Let me hold lightly temporal things,
I who am deathless, I, who wear wings.
Let me hold fast, Lord, things of the skies,
Quicken my vision, open my eyes!
Show me thy riches, glory and grace,
Soundless as time is, endless as space!
Let me hold lightly things that are mine,
Lord thou hast given me All that is Thine!

— *Martha Nicholson*

(143)   Checking the Preachers

A little girl, attending an annual conference session with her mother, watched as her father and other ministerial candidates kneeled before the bishop in an ordination service. The bishop laid his hands on the head of each minister as he gave the commission to preach. "What does that mean?" asked the little girl.

"It is just a ritual," answered the mother, "to impress upon them that their call to preach comes directly from God."

"Oh," said the little girl, "I thought he might be feeling their heads to see if they had any brains before he sent them out to preach."

(144)   The Fruit of Brotherhood

The Communist error is to believe that if all people

share the same property, they will therefore be brothers. This is a grave fallacy: sharing the same apple does not make men brothers, but if men are brothers, they will share the same apple.

— *Bishop Fulton J. Sheen*

(145)   ***No Need to Worry***

In the early part of the century, a Yankee preacher came down to Florida to organize a new church in a rural area. He came up against much opposition from the older resident ministers who didn't trust strangers with new ideas. One day, the Yankee minister, trying to escape the oppressive heat and humidity, decided to take a swim in a small, cool-looking lake. A local preacher was sitting on the bank fishing, and the Yankee asked the good brother if he might take a swim.

"Shore," said the local minister, "I reckon' nobody'll mind if you go on the other side where you won't scare the fish."

"How about snakes," the Yankee preacher asked, "are there any snakes in the lake?"

"Nope, no snakes in this lake," said the fishing preacher, "you go right on ahead and take your swim."

The Yankee preacher was a little surprised at the friendliness of the Florida preacher, because he had been one of those who had shown the young man the most opposition, but he chucked off his clothes on the other side of the lake and dived into the water. He had been swimming for only a minute when he noticed some ripples in the water. They seemed to be moving toward him.

"Hey," he yelled to the Florida preacher, "are you sure there are no snakes in here?"

"Nope, no snakes in there," called the other preacher.

The ripples were getting closer and the Yankee was getting nervous. "How do you know there are no snakes in here?" he yelled a little frantically to the calm fisherman.

"I know there are no snakes in there," the preacher called back, "cause the alligators ate 'em all up!"

— *Selected*

(146) **Active Members**

"How many members do you have in this church?" asked the visiting evangelist.

"Exactly two-hundred," answered the pastor.

"Are they all active?"

"They sure are. One-hundred working for me, and one-hundred working against me!"

(147) **Don't Tell the Missus!**

A city preacher, visiting in the country, decided to do some evangelistic work. Walking through the countryside, he stopped at the gate of a small farmer who was digging in his garden.

"I say," said the preacher, "are you a Christian?"

"Nope," answered the farmer, still digging. "Christian lives up the road a piece."

"What I mean is, are you lost?"

"Well, I reckon' not," answered the farmer, barely looking up, "I've lived in these parts all my life."

"You don't understand," said the exasperated preacher, "Are you ready for Judgment Day?"

"When's it comin?"

"Well, I don't really know, but maybe today, and maybe tomorrow."

"For goodness sakes," said the old farmer, finally looking up from his digging, "don't tell my missus, 'cause she'd want to go both days!"

(148)   **Answered Prayer**

He who rises from prayer a better man, has his prayer answered.

— *George Meredith*

(149)   **Brother Smith's Example**

At a preaching seminar, the visiting evangelist was speaking of the ease with which people are influenced by others for either good or the bad, stressing the need for a positive witness by the servants of God in their daily life and work. Immediately upon finishing his sermon, the preacher stated that there would be a short break after which he would accept comments from the group. Then he dashed for the outside door, where he hastily smoked two cigarettes before resuming his place before the ministers.

The pastor of the host church was sitting at the rear of the sanctuary, struggling with feelings both of anger and embarrassment at the evangelist's actions. Wanting to indicate his opposition, but too kind to embarrass the visiting preacher, he rose to his feet with these words:

"Brother Smith, I just wanted you to know that I am grateful to you for the very graphic illustration you have lent your sermon on witnessing by the extremely brilliant smoking lesson. This example of how we may adversely affect our brethren by bad habits was a masterful 'finish' to your fine sermon, and I will eagerly await your next workshop tomorrow for an imaginative example of how we might *favorably* witness to our people!"

(150) **A Living Thief**

A minister once asked a man why he did not join the church. The man replied that the dying thief did not join the church, and he was saved. "Well," said the minister, "if you do not belong to a church, you do give to missions, don't you?"

"No," said the man, "the dying thief did not help missions and he was saved, wasn't he?"

"Yes," said the minister, "I suppose he was, but you must remember that he was a dying thief, whereas you are a living one."

— *The Christian Herald*

(151) **See Yourself**

Be sure to keep a mirror always nigh, in some convenient, handy sort of place, and now and then look squarely in thine eye, and with thyself keep ever face to face.

— *John Kendrick Bangs*

(152) **A False Contentment**

When neither their property nor honor is touched, the majority of men live content.

— *Niccolo Machiavelli*

(153)   **The Long Reach of God**

A man needs only a short arm to reach to heaven, as heaven is always reaching out to man.

— *Francis Thompson*

(154)   **The Preacher: Spokesman for Christ**

The preacher is the man Christ left to say his words to men. He is to say the thing Christ would say if he were here. The preacher's significant business is with preaching salvation for each man's life. The pulpit is not by calling a civic function. It is a voice from heaven, therefore his ministry is not primarily civic, not primarily for the state. The preacher is a citizen. He ought to love his country, but he is loyal to God first. He votes, but does not let anyone tell him what ticket to vote. He does not preach politics. It is easy for a preacher to think his particular kind of politics a type of religion. It is not. No politics are anything but politics. He is to teach with never a variation the doctrine that the sole way to make a good State is to have regenerated citizens, and that Christ in us is not only the hope of glory, but the hope of the earth.

— *William Quayle*

(155)   **As It Was**

At its first General Conference in 1792, held in Baltimore, Maryland, the Methodist Church set preacher salaries at sixty-four dollars yearly, with the provision that they could claim as expenses the shoes provided for their horses.

(156)   **Appearances Are Not Important**

At the Methodist Conference of 1808, Presiding Elder William McKendree, wearing traditional western clothes, got up to speak; he was so forceful in his delivery that his vest and trousers began to part company, exposing a wide expanse of red underwear. The event did not adversely influence the other preachers, however, because McKendree was elected bishop a few days later.

(157)   **The First Ride — Little Faith**

A preacher took his eighty-five-year-old grandfather on his first plane ride. During the entire trip, the man gripped the arms of the seat in a half-sitting, half-standing position.

"Relax, grandpa," urged the preacher, "try to relax."

"I'm fine," said the old man, "but you're crazy if you think I'm going to put my whole weight on this infernal machine."

(158)   **A Smart Boy**

Visiting a Sunday church school class, the preacher asked a little boy if he knew when the church was founded.

"Founded?" asked the little boy. "I didn't know it was losted."

(159)   **The True Church**

I am the church. You are the church. This is the

church. We are the church — the church dwelling in the heart of the individual, the congregation. The true Church is the Spirit of God working among and within Christ-led people of every race and every nation. And the true church is that church that is faithful to the loving example of Jesus Christ. The true church is not determined by any human founder. Neither is it determined by a mode of baptism, a manner of praying, or a particular method of Communion. The true church is not identified by a name on a building, by an act of worship, or by any physical act or visible sign.

The true church is recognized in the individual and in the congregation when they emit and send forth a power that spreads the joy of sin-forgiveness through the hearts of people. The true church is that church which seeks to replace the hate of the world with the love of Christ.

The true church is that individual, that congregation, who seeks with all of life's being to draw nearer to God and to transmit that radiant, peaceful, and eternal nearness to all the world — with Jesus Christ as example and Lord!

(160)   *Inspiration from Artichokes*

French artist Henri Matisse, when asked where he got the inspiration for painting, answered, "I grow artichokes. Every morning I go in the garden and watch the light and shadows on the artichoke leaves, where I discover new combinations of colors and patterns. I study them, they inspire me, and I go back to the studio and paint."

— *Selected*

(161)   **How Can She Pray?**

A story is told of a little girl whose father was appointed ambassador to West Germany. On the first night after moving to their new home, the little girl prepared to say her prayers. Her mother bowed her head and waited, but the little girl hesitated. Finally the mother asked what was wrong, and the little girl looked up with a sad bewilderment and said, "Mother, I don't know how to pray in German."

(162)   **A Bigger Picture**

A psychiatrist had been treating a woman for many months and was convinced that the greatest problem the woman had was that of her inflated ego and extreme selfishness. Finally he told her, "I can do little for you but advise you to take a trip to the Grand Canyon to see something bigger than yourself."

— *Selected*

(163)   **The Strength of a Child**

A little boy, helping his father prepare a new garden for planting, pulled an old cornstalk from the soft earth.

"Look, daddy," the little boy said excitedly, "I pulled a cornstalk all by myself!"

"Yes," said his father, "you're a strong boy!"

"Yes," said the little boy, "and the whole world was pulling at the other end!"

(164)   *To Seek and to Save*

Many of us are familiar with George Whitefield, the famous preacher and companion of John Wesley, but seldom have we heard of George Whitefield's brother. He had been a devout Christian, but somehow had drifted away and become involved in the pleasures of sin.

One day he heard his brother preach and the sermon deeply touched his heart. The next day he was sitting at tea with the devout Lady Huntingdon, when in the midst of the conversation, a pained look came upon Whitefield's face and he suddenly cried out, "I am a lost man!"

"What did you say, Mr. Whitefield?" asked the startled lady.

"I said I am a lost man," said Whitefield.

"I am glad of it," the lady answered.

"How can you say such a cruel thing?" asked Whitefield.

"I am glad of it," she said, "because it is written, 'The Son of man came to seek and to save that which *is lost.'* "

"What a wonderful Scripture," said the anguished Whitefield, "and how it comes to me with such force. Lady Huntingdon, I thank God for that Scripture and for you. I know now that he has forgiven me and will save me!"

Whitefield walked out of the house rejoicing. He had not gotten out of the courtyard of the house when he fell ill to the ground and shortly thereafter he died.

— *Selected*

(165) **Too Much Hay**

A minister finally got to his church one snowy Sunday to find that he would be joined by only one parishioner, an old farmer who lived nearby.

"Well," the minister said with a smile, "what shall we do?"

"I don't have much education and I don't know much about the Bible," said the farmer, "but I do know that when I promise my cows a load of hay and only one shows up, I feed him."

The minister pulled out his sermon and began to preach — and preach — and preach. Finally he stopped and asked the farmer what he thought of the sermon.

"Well," said the old man, "I don't have much education and I don't know much about the Bible, but I do know that when I promise a load of hay to my cows and only one shows up, I don't give it the whole load!"

(166) **Not the Usual Luxury**

A preacher was holding a revival in a depressed area of the state and was given lodging at the home of a church deacon who was also one of the poorest members of the church. After supper, he was shown to his bed which consisted of a pallet on the floor of the attic. "We're sorry we don't have better quarters," said the deacon's wife. "If there's anything you want, let us know and we'll show you how to get along without it."

(167) **"Hit 'im Again, Lord!"**

The church was in very bad condition and the members were trying to raise money for a new sanctuary. At a board meeting, they began to offer their donations. "I'll give ten dollars," volunteered one. "I'll give twenty-five," said another. "I'll give forty," spoke a third. A very rich, but very stingy member sat in the front row. "I'll give five dollars," he mumbled. Suddenly a large chunk of ceiling fell and hit the stingy one on the head. He immediately jumped up, yelling, "Fifty dollars! I meant fifty dollars!"

A man in the rear of the church spoke out, "Hit 'im again, Lord, hit 'im again!"

(168)   **Each a Part of the Whole**

No man is an island, entire of itself; every man is a piece of the continent, a part of the maine. If a clod be washed away by the sea, Europe is the less as well as if a mountain were washed away. Any man's death diminishes me because I am involved in mankind; and never send to know for whom the bell tolls; it tolls for thee.

— *John Donne*

(169)   **Keepers of the Aquarium**

With all of our education, our theology, our fine buildings, our image of the church, we are doing less to win people to Christ than our unschooled forefathers did. We are no longer fishers of men, but keepers of the aquarium, and we spend most of our time swiping fish from each other's bowl.

— *Dr. Kermit Long*

(170)   *That's the Greatest!*

Two boys were arguing about their father's greatness. "Mine's greater than yours!"
"No he isn't! Ever hear of the Rocky Mountains? My dad built them!"
"That's nothing! Ever hear of the Dead Sea? My dad killed it!"

(171)   *He Wins the Apple*

A theological instructor was sitting next to a young boy on a subway and noted that the youngster was holding a Bible and Sunday church school quarterly on his lap. He decided to have a little fun with the boy. "Tell me, sonny," he asked, "where God is and I'll give you an apple."
The boy looked up at the instructor and promptly replied, "I will give you a whole barrel full of apples if you will tell me where God is not."

— *Selected*

(172)   *Put Your Money Where Your Heart Is*

A group of ministers were sitting over coffee one day when the subject of a fellow minister came up. "John is really having a rough time," said one. "His church is so small they can't afford to pay him much anyway, and with John in the hospital, they are having to pay for a guest speaker every Sunday. "
"Yeah," said another, "and I feel for his wife and kids. I hear she's trying to get a job at the carry-out."

"Well," said still another, "I feel sorry for them too, but I have a few problems . . ."

"I feel that my church can spare me for a couple of Sundays to preach for John," interrupted another, "and I also feel one hundred dollars for him. How do the rest of you feel?"

(173)   *Now You've Gone Too Far!*

An older Christian, in charge of the church stewardship program, asked a new convert, "If you had one hundred sheep, would you give half to the Lord's work?"

"Yes," answered the new convert.

"If you had one hundred horses or one hundred cows, would you give half to the Lord's work?"

"Yes, of course," answered the new convert.

"If you had two pigs, would you give half to the Lord's work?" persisted the stewardship worker.

"No!" answered the new convert. "And you have no right to ask because you know I have two pigs!"

(174)   *One More Thing You Can Do*

A little girl was taken to a department store to see Santa Claus. She told Santa all the things she wanted: a doll, dishes, clothes, a tricycle, and more. Then Santa gave her a big apple. The mother said to the little girl, "Now what do you say to Santa?"

The little girl thrust the apple at Santa and answered, "Peel it!"

(175)   **A Christian**

Faith makes a Christian. Life proves a Christian. Trial confirms a Christian. Death crowns a Christian.

— *J. Ellis*

(176)   **"I'll Just Put My Hand In His"**

The minister was visiting a saintly church member who was suffering from an incurable disease. Trying to comfort her, the minister found that he was the one who was comforted.

"As a child," the woman said, "I remember my mother showing me a picture of Jesus leading little children. Now I'll be just like a child and put my hand in his, and he will lead me home."

(177)   **Quite a Dilemma**

A preacher saw a small newsboy standing on a corner crying, and stopped to ask him what was wrong.

"Preacher, I can't read and I forgot what I'm supposed to holler!"

(178)   **True Charity**

True charity is not just giving a man a dime when he is hungry. It is giving a man a dime when you are as hungry as he is and need the dime just as badly.

— *Gandhi*

(179) **A Little Mixed Up**

In a Sunday church school class, the teacher was speaking about kindness to animals and thought it would be nice if the students shared some information about their pets. "I have a dog," volunteered a small boy. "What kind is it?" the teacher asked him. "Oh, he's a mixed-up kind — sort of a cocker scandal."

(180) **Expectation**

Many preachers and church workers complain regularly because Sunday services seem so lifeless and uneventful. Perhaps, suggest others, nothing happens because we don't expect anything to happen. The day that Christians come together in great faith and with great expectations, is the day that they will feel the tremendous outpouring of the Holy Spirit.

— *Selected*

(181) **A Lesson from Gettysburg Hannah**

It is said that during the battle of Gettysburg, when the armies of the North and the South came together in the little Pennsylvania town, one of Gettysburg's citizens, a woman named Hannah, met the rebels with a broom in her hand. Questioned later, she said, "I wanted them to know which side I'm on!"

(182) **An Epitaph**

The day before he died, Daniel Webster dictated this

epitath for his grave:

Philosophical argument, especially that drawn from the vastness of the universe, in comparison with the apparent insignificance of this globe, has sometimes shaken my reason for the faith which is in me; but my heart has always assured me that the gospel of Jesus Christ must be Divine Reality. The Sermon on the Mount cannot be a mere human production. This belief enters into the very depth of my conscience. The whole history of man proves it.

(183)   **Deceptive Appearances**

Just after a destructive flood hit the area, I was driving through a small Eastern Kentucky town and remarked to my wife that it was one of the most depressing places I had ever seen. How awful it would be to live in such a place, I thought.

I did not see the town again until five years later — the day I was transferred there! It was with great misgiving that I accepted the move, and determined that the stay would be as short as possible.

Our residence there was all too short. When I was transferred once again, we left with much reluctance. We had grown to love the beauty of the mountains, the sometimes wild Kentucky River which flowed nearby, and the unhurried pace of life in the small town. But most of all, we were reluctant to leave the people who had become warm and gracious friends that we will always remember with great affection.

To judge anything or anyone by first appearance is not only foolish, but it may also prevent you from enjoying some of God's finest places — and people.

(184)   *Just in Case*

It is told that when a famous agnostic comedian was lying on his deathbed, he was visited by a friend who found the comedian reading a Bible.

"I thought you didn't believe in the Bible," said the friend.

"I don't," said the comedian. "I'm just looking for loopholes."

(185)   *Leaky Books*

A missionary had a great fondness for rich red wine, and he regularly had a friend ship him a case to the remote area which he was serving in Alaska — marking the crate as containing books. One day he received a message from the station-master which read, "Reverend, you'd better come down here soon and pick up your shipment. Your books are leaking."

(186)   *Tell It Like It Is*

At a revival meeting, a man got up, rambling on, and on, and on about his past sins until most of the people were getting a little tired. "I've done every contemptible thing," the man said, "that anyone could do. I've been a contemptible swine, but I never knew it before tonight!"

"Oh, sit down," said a weary man on the front row. The rest of us knew it all the time."

(187)   *Can't They Hear What I'm Saying?*

The church board sent a spokesman to the minister.

"Preacher, I've been asked to speak to you about your sermons — or I guess I should say sermon since you've been preaching the same one every Sunday. Can't you come up with a new one?"

"I'll be glad to," said the preacher, "when the people start listening to this one."

(188)   **She Set the Example**

At a church pot-luck dinner, the visiting evangelist was talking to one of the members. "By whose preaching were you converted?" he asked the young man.

"By no one's preaching," came the answer, "but by my mother's example."

(189)   **Protect Your Middle**

A preacher was bragging to another about his unshakeable faith. "I keep my head in the heavens and my feet firmly planted on the earth."

"That's fine," said the other, "but what if life hits you around the belt buckle?"

(190)   **Only One Step to God**

During World War Two, a young Dutch patriot was captured by the Nazis and sentenced to die. The night before the execution, the young boy wrote a letter to his parents in these words:

Dear Father, it is difficult for me to write this letter to you, but I have to tell you that the military court has promised a very heavy sentence on me. Read this letter alone and then tell Mother carefully. In a little while, at five o'clock, it is going to happen, and that is not so terrible. I do not fear. I have the firm conviction that I may look forward to death in Christ. It is, after all, only one moment and then I shall be with God. I am courageous, be the same. They can only take our bodies, our souls are in God's hands. May God bless you all. Have not hate. I die without hatred. God rules everything.

— Told by John Clark

(191)   **Let Your Light Shine**

In England there is a chapel which has unusually small stained glass windows. The effect of this is a very dark sanctuary. However, each worshiper is given a candle upon entering, and thus brings his own bit of light into the darkness.

(192)   **Beyond**

Beyond the door there is a fireplace,
Beyond the night there breaks the dawn;
And there is beauty in the sunrise
Beyond the room where shades are drawn.

Beyond the clouds there is the sunshine,
Beyond the storm the quiet calm;
And beyond the winter's silence
Spring bursts forth in joyous song.

Beyond today there lies tomorrow,
Beyond tomorrow, eternity;
Beyond death the resurrection
Through Christ who died for you and me.

Beyond the world of sin and sorrow,
If to God we now respond,
Is the city of perfection
Where we no more shall look beyond.

— *Edith Cawood*

(193)   ***Hypocritical Hymn Singing***

We sing "Sweet Hour of Prayer" and are content with five or ten minutes a day (or less).

We sing "Onward Christian Soldiers" and wait to be drafted into His service.

We sing "O For A Thousand Tongues To Sing" and don't use the one we have (or use it in the wrong way.)

We sing "There Shall Be Showers of Blessings" but will not go to church when it rains.

We sing "Blest Be The Tie That Binds" and let the least little offense sever it.

We sing "I Love To Tell The Story" and never mention it at all.

We sing "Cast Thy Burden On the Lord" and worry ourselves into nervous breakdowns.

We sing "O Day of Rest And Gladness" but wear ourselves out traveling, fishing, hunting, or playing golf on Sunday.

— *Bethesda Bulletin*

(194)   A Short Eulogy

At the grave of the departed, the old backwoods preacher stood hat in hand. Looking into the abyss he delivered the brief funeral oration. "Sam Johnson," he said sorrowfully, "you are gone. And we shore hopes you are gone where we thinks you ain't."

— *Selected*

(195)   Reflection

Reflect upon your present blessings of which every man has many; not upon your past misfortunes of which all have some.

— *Charles Dickens*

(196)   The Importance of Example

In Rudyard Kipling's story, *The Convert*, an Indian girl turns to a chaplain's wife for comfort, but the chaplain's wife is not sympathetic and turns the girl away. The Indian girl thus turned against Christianity, saying, "To my own gods I go. It may be they shall give me greater ease than your cold Christ and tangled trinities!"

(197)   All That Is Left

Constantine the Great, in order to bring a selfish miser to the church, took a lance and marked out a space of ground equal to the size of a human body. "Add heap to heap," said Constantine, "accumulate riches upon riches, extend the bounds of your possessions, conquer the whole world, and in a few days such a spot as this will be all you will have."

— *Selected*

(198)   **When the Light Goes Out**

A man was injured in an accident and the doctor told him that he could eventually lose his sight. One day, while at work, the man found that his sight was rapidly fading and he called for his son. "Son," he said, "you had better come and get me. The lights are going out."

"Don't worry, Dad," said the son. "I'll be your light from now on. You will see through my eyes."

The light of every human being will one day fade, but can be revived again by the one who says, "I am the light of the world: he that followeth me shall not walk in darkness, but shall have the light of life." (John 8:12)

— *Selected*

(199)   **A Little Sacrifice at a Time**

Near the turn of the present century, a Methodist church in Whitley City, Kentucky was assigned a preacher who was convinced that tobacco in any form was a chief tool of the devil. He had not been in Whitley City long before he discovered that many of his parishioners disagreed with him, and were addicted to both the growing and the using of the weed.

Needless to say, the parson had quite a few words to say about the tobacco tipplers, but his listeners merely stepped up the pace of their dipping, chomping, and puffing. Not to be discouraged, the persistent preacher continued his verbal barrages against the tobacco target, and one Sunday, he was convinced that he had won the battle.

That Lord's Day, after a particularly forceful sermon in which he urged the imbibers to sacrifice by giving up their tobacco, he was pleasantly surprised during the offertory to see the collection plates being returned to the altar heaped high with plugs of tobacco, tubes of snuff, and sacks of *Bull Durham*.

The parson was sure his victory had been won. After the service, the treasurer reported that the people had indeed given up their tobacco, but they had apparently decided that one sacrifice was enough — so they kept their money.

— *Pulpit To Pew*

(200)   **To God Be the Glory**

To God be the glory, Who created all things;
A volcano raging, a bluebird that sings,
The smile of a baby, the dew on a rose,
For refreshing our bodies, with a calm night's repose.

To God be the glory, Who created and gave;
Us an earth filled with wonder, from birth to the grave,
For in God's endless universe, no tongue can proclaim,
The infinite greatness of His Holy Name.

— *Grace Davis*

(201)   **Amen**

In the heat of the church, the sermon went on, and on, and on. Finally the minister paused. "What more, my friends, can I say?"

From the back of the church came a hushed, but emphatic answer: *"Amen!"*

Subject Index

A Abraham (84); Accounts (86); Adam (84); Adoration (99); Aerodynamics (2); Agnosticism (184); Alone (76); Alpha (66); Appearances (25), (156), (183); Amen (2OI); Arizona (84); Artichokes (160); Astronomy (1); Atheism (127); Auctioneer (75);

B Backsliding (114); Beauty (55); Beecher, Henry Ward (13); Beginning (1), (66); Beyond (192); Birds (71); Bishops (121), (143); Boat (70); Books (185); Brains (143); Brothers, Brotherhood (37), (54), (144); Bullsnake (12); Bumblebee (2); Burma Buddhists (23);

C California (84); Calling (103); Caring (102); Change (119); Children (4), (6), (27), (34), (46), (49), (58), (59), (69), (93), (108), (110), (117), (128), (143), (158), (161), (163), (170), (171), (174), (177), (179); Christian (84), (89); Christian Influence (85); Christmas (54), (63); Church Attendance (6), (23), (64), (78), (82), (98), (122), (165); Church Collection (4), (90); Church Membership (13), (14), (47), (109); Cities (85); Clock (19); Communication (106); Communism (144); Compassion (63); Complacency (92); Computers (10); Condemnation (55); Confession (112); Consecration (141); Constantine the Great (197); Courage (54); Creation (1), (10), (64), (66); Cross (124); Crucifixion of Christ (110); Cuba (5), (99);

D Deacons (166); Death (28), (36), (39), (42), (46), (119), (175), (176), (194); Deeds (81); Denominations (82); Dentists (93); Destructiveness (50); Devil (47); Devotion (131), (137); Dishes (24); Dogs (131), (179); Donne, John (168); Drifting (71); Dust (46);

E Editor (86); Enemy (57); Epitaph (182); Erasures (138); Eternal Life (36), (87); Evangelists (149), (188); Evangelization (109), (169); Eve (84); Exaggeration (24); Example (30), (196); Expectation (180);

F Faith (2), (5), (11), (35), (43), (49), (70), (127), (175), (176), (190); Faithfulness (131); Farmer (86), (147), (165), (173); Fear (56), (62), (97); Feuding (89); Fishing (73); Flight (2); Florida (84); Footprints (125); Forgiveness (48), (57), (97);

G Gambling (114); Gettysburg Hannah (181); Gospel (7), (140); Gossip (21), (68), (79); Graham, Billy (104); Gratitude (80); Gravestone (28), (52);

H Hatred (Lack of) (190); Haydon, Robert (100); Heart (74); Heavens (1), (126), (153); Hope (54); Horse (13); Hospital (54); Hypocrite (133), (193);

I Ignorance (115); Illness (22); Influence (7), (8), (9), (19), (20), (30), (54), (89); Innocence (of Children) (108); Inspiration (160);

J Jesus (22), (60), (64), (66), (72), (73), (75); Johnson, Samuel (119);

K Kentucky (84); Kindness (51), (54);

L Lamb, Charles (100); Lee, Robert E. (48); Life (32), (38), (39), (42), (43), (52), (60), (78), (87); Light (20), (34), (56), (191), (198); Lincoln, Abraham (25); Livingstone, David (8); Loopholes (184); Love (30), (41), (57), (66), (78), (190); Luther, Martin (137);

M Marriage (53); Materialism (14); Matheson, George (139); McKendree, Bishop (156); Membership (146); Methodism, Methodist Church (155), (156); Miller, Peter (57); Mind (74); Missionary (185); Missions (150); Money (172); Mosaic Law (94);

N Names (84), (89); Narrow-mindedness (107); Nature of Man (50); Neighbors (41); Newly-weds (111); New Mexico (84); Noise (120);

O Obedience (127), (130); Offering (4); Omega (66), (100); Opinion (48); Optimism (44); Owl (103);

P Paul (22), (33), (84); Pardon (57); Pennsylvania (84); Perception (128); Peter (84), (130); Phylactery (94); Pleasure (27); Politicians (31); Pope, Alexander (107); Prayer (33), (106), (123), (128), (133), (135), (148), (161); Preachers, Preaching (3), (9), (15), (24), (29), (53), (79), (90), (95), (116), (120), (128), (143), (145), (147), (149), (154), (187), (188), (189), (194), (199); Presence of God (76), (104); Priest (11); Protestant (11); Psychiatrists (162);

R Rabbi (11); Reason (35); Relaxation (157); Religion (43); Reminiscing (27); Renewal (16), (81); Repentance (81); Responsibility (63); Resurrection (110); Revival (103), (114), (166), (186); Riches (142); Righteousness, Unrighteousness (133);

S Sacrifice (199); Saint Francis (9); Salvation (164); Samaritans (63); Samuel (84); Santa (54), (174); Satan (21); Selfishness (162), (167); Sermon (116); Sheen, Bishop Fulton J. (144); Skepticism (72); Smoking (149); Soul (74); Speaking (77); Spurgeon, Charles (7); Stanley, Henry (8); Stars (64), (117), (118); Stewardship (167), (173); Strength (22), (74), (97); Stubborness (12); Substitution (29); Symbolism (113);

T Taxes (91); Teachers (117); Teenagers (105), (134); Temptation (30); Thief (150); Time (18), (19); Timidity (132); Tobacco (199); Today (62); Tomb (36); Tomorrow (62), (129); Train (3); Tribute (45), (102); Trust in God (88); Truth (66);

U Universe (117), (118), (200);

V Victory (61); Violin (75); Visions (137); Voice of God (40);

W Wandering (71); Washington, George (57); Weakness (22); Webster, Daniel (182); West Virginia (84); Whitefield, George (164); Will, Willpower (39); Wisdom (33); Witness (7), (8), (9); Wonders of God (64); Works (6), (49), (70); World War Two (69), (190); Worship (99);

Y Yesterday (62)